RUTH MINSKY SENDER
the cage

Simon Pulse

First paperback edition August 1997

Aladdin Paperbacks
An imprint of Simon & Schuster
Children's Publishing Division
1230 Avenue of the Americas
New York, NY 10020

Also available in a Simon & Schuster Books for Young Readers edition.

Designed by Leslie Tane
The text of this book was set in 12.5 point Berkely Oldstyle.

Manufactured in the United States of America

22 24 25 23

The Library of Congress has cataloged the hardcover edition as follows:
Sender, Ruth Minsky.
The cage.
Summary: A teenage girl recounts the suffering and persecution of her family under the Nazis—in a Polish ghetto, through deportation, and in concentration camps.
1. Holocaust, Jewish (1939–1945)—Poland—Lódź—Personal narratives—Jewish literature. 2. Sender, Ruth Minsky—Juvenile literature.
[1. Holocaust, Jewish (1939–1945)—Poland—Lódź—Personal narratives. 2. Sender, Ruth Minsky] I. Title.
D810.J4S397   1986
940.53'15'03924024   86-8562
ISBN-10: 0-02-781830-6 (hc.)

ISBN-13: 978-0-689-81321-4 (pbk.)
ISBN-10: 0-689-81321-X (pbk.)

To all those who perished in silent resistance,
a memorial.

To all those who rose from the ashes and built
a new life,
a tribute.

To my children,
for giving me the strength to continue.

WHY?

Written by Riva Minska,
Number 55082
Camp Mittelsteine, Germany
January 14, 1945

Translated from the Yiddish
by Ruth Minsky Sender, Free Person
New York City, U.S.A.
1980

All alone, I stare at the window
Feeling my soul in me cry
Hearing the painful screams of my heart
Calling silently: Why?
Why are your dreams scattered, destroyed?
Why are you put in this cage?
Why is the world silently watching?
Why can't they hear your rage?
Why is the barbed wire holding me prisoner
Blocking to freedom my way?
Why do I still keep waiting and dreaming

Hoping . . . maybe . . . someday . . .
I see above me the snow-covered mountains
Majestic, proud, and high
If like a free bird I could reach their peaks
Maybe from there the world will hear my cry . . .
Why?

PART
ONE

PART ONE

1

Warm rays of sunshine fill the house, mixed with the sweet smell of lilac in full bloom. Cheerful sounds of chirping birds reach my ears. A gentle breeze coming through the open window caresses my face. It is spring. It is good to be alive. I feel calm and happy this morning.

I had no nightmares last night. I slept well. No screams, no moans, no cries for help. Restful sleep. It happens so very, very seldom.

The nightmares fill most of my nights and stay with me through most days. I try hard not to think about them. Keep my mind busy. Remember the joys in my life, my children.

And then night comes. My yesterdays are back again. They become today. My children are in my dreams. I am a child myself and also a mother. I run from the Nazis, and my children are with me. I try to hide them from the Nazis. I know I must hide them to save them, but I have no place to run to. The Nazis are all around us. They point their rifles at us. They reach out to take away my children. I hear their commands: "Jews, out! Jews, out!" I hear my voice, filled with horror: "Not again! Not again!"

I wake up screaming. I sit up dazed, shaken, my body covered with cold sweat. I feel my husband's arms around me, pressing me close to him. We do not speak, only hold each other tight. He also wakes up screaming at night. He is the only survivor of his family, and he knows my nightmares.

I lie awake now, still trembling. The faces of my mother, brothers, aunts, uncles, cousins, teachers, friends float before my eyes. A long procession of faces, some sharp and clear, some hidden behind a cloudy veil. Faces of people I loved, cherished, respected. They were all part of my life. Now they are all dead. Murdered. Not a trace left. Not even a grave.

Suddenly a through unfolds in my mind. A revelation. My children carry some of their names. These are the children who, according to the Nazi master plan to annihilate all the Jews, were not to be born. Their parents were to die, like the six million of their Jewish brothers and sisters who died in gas chambers,

2

crematoriums, lonely hiding places. But we survived and gave them life. Here they are, the Jewish generation that was not to be, proud human beings, the new link in an old chain.

I fall asleep again, calmed. But the nightmares return. I am forever running, hiding, screaming.

Today, with the sun so bright, the air filled with sweet smells of spring, the happy sounds of birds singing, all my nightmares seem unreal. If they were real, would the sun shine so brightly? Would the birds sing so happily? Would I smile?

I look through the open front door. My daughter, Nancy, is playing in the grass, the new green grass, sprouting again from the earth that was cold and frozen all winter. New life is growing all around me, reaching toward the sun. My child: happy, healthy, strong, blossoming like a beautiful flower.

Suddenly Nancy is near me. She cuddles up to me, and I put my arms around her, pulling her close. I see the sadness in her face and ask softly, "What is wrong, sweetheart?" I know that look. I have seen it many times in the eyes of my sons, when they come upon something that brings back painful memories to me. They try to protect me from them.

I kiss her gently. She hesitates, then in a broken voice says, "I saw my friend's grandparents. It made me feel so sad." Tears fill my eyes. It is not the first time I have heard that. My children have never felt the joy and love of grandparents. "Why, Mommy? Why? Why did the Nazis kill them, my grandparents?"

She is only a child. How do I answer her? "The Nazis were evil. They wanted the world only for themselves. They killed your grandparents, my family, Daddy's family, six million of our people only because we were Jews."

Nancy looks at me, bewildered. "Why did they let them do it? Why didn't people stop them?"

Why did they let them do it? Why did they let them do it? It echoes in my ears. Many voices ring in my ears. Voices I have heard before. They are all calling, *Why? Why? Why did they let them do it?*

I hear Mama's voice, filled with hope. *A world full of people will not be silent. We will not perish in vain.* She was so sure. But she perished, and the world was silent.

4

Tears fall down my face. Nancy's soft hands wipe them away. "But, Mommy, it could not happen here. Our neighbors, our friends, they would help."

Suddenly it is 1939 again.

2

Lodz, Poland.

It is spring. The smell of fresh paint blends with the fresh scent of the new season. Spring, warm and gentle, brings the beautiful holiday of freedom: *Pesach*, or Passover.

The hustle of Pesach is in full swing. The homes are aired, cleaned, and painted. Excitement is in the air. The long-awaited guest is coming to remind us of the joys of freedom and the bitterness of slavery.

Mama is busy sewing new clothes for her seven children. Pesach would not be the same without new clothes and new shoes. She sings a Yiddish song, pushing the pedal of the sewing machine to the rhythm of the tune:

> Tell me, children, if you know,
> What is this dear holiday called?

Her song and the sound of the sewing machine ring happily all through the house.

6

the cage

Mrs. Gruber, our landlady, pokes her silver-gray head through the open door of our apartment. "Nacha," she calls in her rugged voice, "don't forget to order your matzos today. The holiday is almost here! I see you still have a lot to do to get ready!" Her eyes take in every little detail of our busy home and stop to rest for a moment on the table laden with all kinds of fabrics. "And remember to make something for my Harry for Pesach!" she adds, still standing by the open door, too busy to come inside.

Mama smiles and calls back. "I ordered matzos already, Mrs. Gruber. I will be ready for Pesach in time, don't worry." From the pile of fabric she picks up black satin and silver braid. "This, Mrs. Gruber, is for your grandson Harry, for his new peasant shirt, the same shirt that I am making for my sons. You know, Harry is one of my kids, too."

Mrs. Gruber smiles her approval, leaving to make the rounds of her other tenants, to make sure they are all ready to greet the holiday with honor. She stops to admire her pride and joy, the huge oak tree in the yard, its strong branches covered with blossoms.

I have the job of cleaning our windows for the holidays, and I see Mrs. Gruber standing under the tree, proud and stately, just like that old oak tree. I see the tree covered with big, green leaves, spreading out its branches like a beautiful umbrella even now, when it is first beginning to sprout.

On hot summer days, I see our tired neighbors sitting in the tree's shade, trying to solve the problems of the world. It is so much easier to solve world problems in the shade of a huge oak tree. I often hear them say, "What pleasure, such a tree."

I look at Mrs. Gruber again. I am thirteen years old, and I have known her all my life. My mother was born in this house, and Olga, Mrs. Gruber's daughter, was also born here. Olga's thirteen-year-old son, Harry, is like a member of my family. I have brothers and sisters, but Harry is an only child and spends most of his time with us.

They all speak Yiddish, celebrate the holidays with us, share our lives. It is hard to believe they are not Jewish. They are so much a part of our world, in happiness and in sorrow. If one of us takes sick, Mrs. Gruber is the first to come running with her remedies and treats. If we play too loudly, she is the first to scold us: "Slow down, you'll break a leg. Your mother has plenty to worry about without you kids giving her more trouble!"

Mama is a widow, supporting seven young children. She runs a tailor factory and works very hard to be able to send us to private schools. She gives us the best she can in a home filled with love. We are all happy, surrounded by friends we can trust and count on.

The lovely Pesach passes, and spring turns into summer.

The discussions under the oak tree are loud and full of worry. Words like *war* and *Hitler* are part of the daily vocabulary. Reserve soldiers are being recalled for duty. It is believed to be only a precaution.

"Poland is strong!" I hear Moishe, our neighborhood optimist. "We have nothing to worry about. The world will not let Hitler take over Poland."

"But the world let Hitler take over Austria and Czechoslovakia." Yankl voices his view.

Harry and I sit on the grass near the tree

and listen. I am frightened as I look at the faces of our neighbors. Their eyes are so full of fear and sadness. They know war brings hunger, pain, death. . . .

I look at Harry. Our eyes meet. Silently we take each other's hand. Harry's gentle touch makes me feel safer. Why would anybody want to hurt us? We are only children. No reason to be afraid. No reason to panic.

But panic and hysteria slowly take over. Stories about German spies, rumors about traitors among the people spread like fire out of control.

One day an angry mob surrounds Harry, shouting, "He is a spy! He is sending secrets to the Germans! He is a German! His ancestors were Germans! Kill him! Kill him!"

Harry's face is pale and stricken with terror. He is begging, "Let me go. Don't hurt me. I am not a spy! Please!"

I see Harry pushed against the wall, his shirt torn. I scream, "Leave him alone! He is my brother. He is not a German. You are all mad!"

They are mad. They do not know what they are doing. They will hurt my friend. I know he is not a spy.

the cage

I see Mama. Like a tigress pushing forward to protect her young, her eyes flashing, her voice raging, she places herself in front of Harry. "What are you doing?" she shouts. "He is only a child! We all know him. He was born here. Grew up with our children. He is one of us. Our child! You will have to kill me before you touch a hair on his head! Go home and calm down!"

She looks at the faces around her. There is sudden silence. Painful silence. They are leaving.

Mama holds Harry close to her. He is trembling. She whispers gently, "It is over. You are safe now."

Harry is crying. I cry with him. What crazy, crazy people. How could Harry, his mother, his grandmother do anything to hurt us, their friends? Only because they have German ancestors. . . . They are not Germans. They are part of our family.

3

In September 1939, the Germans invade Poland. They march into the homes of Jews, giving them five minutes to move out, beating and killing helpless people. It is war against the Jews: men, women, children.

A new breed of German comes suddenly to life: *Volksdeutsche*. Poles who never knew of their German heritage dig into their past to find a drop of German blood that will link them to "the Fatherland." They put on swastikas and become Nazis.

Mrs. Gruber, Olga, and Harry join the *Volksdeutsche*. Mrs. Gruber loads wagons with Jewish belongings she has taken and moves into a Jewish home in the nicest part of Lodz.

Morning. A pounding at the door. I jump out of my bed, startled. "Open the door!" It is a familiar voice. I open the door. Before me, smiling proudly, stands Harry in the uniform of the Hitler Youth. He holds a club in his hands.

the cage

I stare at him in disbelief. A cold sweat covers my body. I feel sick. "Not you," I whisper hoarsely. "Not you, Harry. How could you join them? How could you, my brother, become a part of killing our people? You know what the Nazis are doing is horrible, unforgivable. . . ."

For a moment he looks a little ashamed. Then a Harry I never knew, in a voice I never heard before, says, "Riva, Germany is my fatherland. I'll do anything for my fatherland."

I feel the salty taste of tears in my mouth. They have poisoned his mind.

"I will still be your friend." His voice is softer now. "I'll help you, protect you." In his new brown uniform, blond, blue-eyed, he looks like the boys on the Nazi posters I have seen.

He touches my hand. I pull away. "Why are you moving away from me?" he asks, bewildered. "Why are you crying?"

"I am crying for both of us, Harry. I am crying for both of us. . . ." I run to my bed and bury my head in the pillow.

Later his family stands calmly by, watching *Volksdeutsche* rob our home. Our tile oven, used to heat the house, attracts Mr. Brown, the farmer who has delivered potatoes to us for many years.

"Mr. Brown." Mama pleads with him with tears in her eyes. "Mr. Brown, it is winter. It is bitter cold. My children will freeze. Please don't take the oven now. I will give it to you as soon as it gets a little bit warmer. But not now, please. We have nothing else to keep the house warm." She stands between him and the oven, begging for her children's sake.

He pushes her roughly aside, puts rope around the oven, ties the rope around himself, and carries the oven to his wagon without saying a word.

"Mrs. Gruber!" Mama calls desperately. "Please stop him! Help me!" Tears pour from her eyes now. "You are my friend. He'll listen to you! Don't let my children freeze!" She turns to Olga. "Please, Olga, have pity! Help me!"

"Don't worry, Nacha," Olga says calmly. "You will not be here much longer. You will all be gone soon."

She walks over to the closet and opens it wide. My Uncle Chaim, a furrier, left several fur coats for safekeeping. She takes the coats and

14

puts them over her shoulder. "You will not need these, either," she says in a chilling voice, walking out the door.

We all stand motionless, shocked, betrayed, helpless.

"You will pay for you crimes!" Mama cried out. "God will punish you for what you are doing! German blood will flow, just as Jewish blood is flowing in the streets! Remember my words, Mrs. Gruber! Remember!"

Mrs. Gruber, her arms filled with our possessions, turns to Mama in a rage. "Be silent! God is with *us*! I could have you killed for your insane outcry, Nacha!"

Mama looks at her in sudden terror. Is this the woman she has known all her life, her friend in happiness and sorrow? "What happened to you? What happened to you?" she whispers.

Standing in the doorway, Mrs. Gruber calls out, "Next week I am sending men to chop down the oak tree. I do not want you Jews to enjoy the beauty of my tree."

"Mrs. Gruber, you took our homes, you took our belongings, you took our pride," Mama says in a strange voice. "Take your tree.

The dead tree will help us remember what you became."

Mrs. Gruber stares at Mama for a moment. Then she turns and walks out.

I run to Mama's arms. "Why did they betray us like this?" I whisper. "Why? Why?"

4

Day by day, more and more Jewish families are thrown out of their homes, robbed of their belongings, their lives. Bearded Jews are pulled from the sidewalk by their beards. With burning cigarettes their beards are put ablaze. Their screams of horror and pain create a spectacle for the Nazis, whose shouts of pleasure drown out the cries of torment.

April 1940. The sky is sunny and bright. The little white clouds, gliding slowly through the clear, blue sky, look so gentle, so pure. The hearts of the people below are heavy.

Saba and I are on our way to the post office to mail a registered letter to our relatives in Argentina. Saba is my cousin and one of my best friends. Her big, brown eyes, always smiling mischievously from under her long, dark eyelashes, today look sad, bewildered. Her sweet, gentle face has become stern and cold. I look at Saba and wonder: Have I changed that much, too?

For a long time we walk in silence, Saba and I, the two who always had so much to say, so much to get excited about—school, clubs, boys—so many plans to make for our future. It is all so far away now, so unimportant. I am thirteen, Saba fifteen. But we are not young anymore.

I glance at Saba, and my eyes pause at the yellow star on her coat. I look at the yellow star on my coat. Around us I see others wearing the yellow star that marks us as Jews.

I take Saba's hand in mine. "Saba, are you ashamed of wearing the yellow star of disgrace?"

She looks at the yellow, six-pointed star a moment, and her eyes light up with pride. "Why should I be?" she asks, holding her head high. "The Star of David is a Jewish symbol, and I am proud to be a Jew! What we are wearing is only a yellow piece of cloth. Let those who make us wear it feel shame."

Suddenly a heavy hand grabs my shoulder with force. A loud voice shouts, "Jews, halt! Off the sidewalk!"

I feel chills running down my spine. My feet feel numb. I cannot move. The cold, piercing eyes of the Nazi cut into my heart. I remain frozen.

One kick of his boot, and I am in the gutter. I see rings before my eyes and seem to be floating like a little white cloud. Slowly I open my eyes. My head hurts. Somebody is helping me up. Around me I see men, women, children, all with the yellow star on their clothing. I look frantically for Saba. I cannot see her. "Saba! Sabcia!" I call. No reply.

The crowd in the street is getting bigger. Women with babies, children carrying schoolbooks, men in work clothes, men in Hasidic garb, all puzzled, frightened, pressing closer and closer together.

From time to time we hear shots, screams, and painful silence again. Through my mind runs a horrible thought: We are going to die. My heart starts pounding violently. Suddenly I imagine Mama's face, gentle and stained with tears. I break out crying. I hear her whispering, *Be brave, my child, be brave.*

Like a revelation, bright and clear, it comes to me. The bravest person I have ever known is Mama. She was a very young woman when my father died suddenly during a typhus epidemic.

She had six young children and was expecting the seventh. My little brother, Avrom Moishe, is named after my father and my grandfather, who also died that same year. I was five then, too young to understand her tragedy. Only now, facing death, I realize what bravery, what courage it took for Mama to go on.

Just a few months ago, Mama helped her three older children, Mala, Chana, and Yankele, pack a few things and sent them away, to be smuggled across the border to Russia. "I'll stay here with the little ones," she said. "I'll keep a home ready until you can return safely. The Germans won't hurt women and young children."

Often I hear her crying at night and whispering softly to herself, "Are they safe? Are they starving? Do they have a roof over their heads? My poor children, could they be lost somewhere in a distant land, homeless, cold, and hungry?"

If she should lose me now . . . I must be brave. I must have hope.

The crowd around me is swelling larger and larger. There are hundreds of people now, surrounded by German soldiers pointing rifles at us.

the cage

"Forward, march!" sounds a German command. "Forward, march!" Hundreds of feet, little feet of small children, heavy feet of men and women, begin a march to the unknown.

"Faster! Faster!" shout the Germans, shooting their rifles over our heads. Screams of panic cut through the air. "Run! Run! Faster! Faster!" Suddenly, "Stop! Stop!" Again, "Run! Run!" and again, "Stop! Stop!" People trample one another.

Before me is an expectant mother. She can hardly catch her breath. A man near her is trying to help her stay on her feet. The German soldier at our side notices this. He jerks the woman out of the line and kicks her from behind. She falls flat on her stomach.

Her horrified screams pierce our hearts. I hear a voice behind me shout, "God in heaven, why are you silent?" Someone reaches out to help the pregnant woman, and his head is split open by a German rifle butt. Blood streaming over his face, he lies near the woman.

We run, stop, run, stop. From a distance I see our neighbor, Mr. Avner, the kind, generous man who buys us treats and chats with us children. He always listens so closely, such a gentle person. I wish I could speak to him now.

"Mr. Avner! Mr. Avner!" I call. He does not hear me. "Mr. Avner! Mr. Avner!" I call again. He turns his head in my direction. He sees me. He shouts something, but I cannot hear him. He points to his short, graying beard and lifts it high. I get the message: chin up. Then I lose sight of him.

I feel someone's hand clutching mine. I turn to my left. The brown, frightened eyes of a little boy look pleadingly at me. His fingers dig into my skin, as if he were trying to attach himself to me, seeking protection from the horrors around him.

He is about ten years old. Under one arm he carries a Hebrew book. He looks like a small, helpless animal caught in a trap. I pull him tighter to my side. Our eyes meet in silent understanding.

"Forward, march!" shout the Germans, strengthening their command with shots.

Run. Stop. Run. Stop. We pass the same streets again and again. They are chasing us in circles. We are still in the same section of Lodz where they herded us together. I hold on tightly to my new little friend. His closeness gives me strength.

the cage

Suddenly I hear familiar, throaty, incoherent sounds behind me. I turn my head. In the crowd, separated from me by many people, I see my deaf-mute friend Abram. His eyes raging with frustration, his arms moving frantically, husky sounds tearing from his throat, he is trying to answer the German who is poking him with his rifle while asking him something.

Abram became my neighbor and friend five months ago. He is sixteen. He has a brother and sister who are also deaf-mutes. I learned to communicate with them and gained their trust. We discovered that their teacher, Mrs. Lichtenstein, whom they all love and respect, is a friend of my family, and I, too, love her. This brought us closer together.

Abram has a keen mind. We speak to each other with pencil and paper. But I also understand the sounds of his silent throat, the sounds I hear now, resentful and bitter.

I am trying to get his attention by waving to him. I know he cannot hear me. Still I call, "Abram! Abram!"

The German is getting angry at him; he will hurt him. I scream: "He is a deaf-mute! Help him, please, help him!"

People around me pass it on. "He is a deaf-mute. He is a deaf-mute."

A woman near Abram pleads with the German: "Please, have pity. Let him be. He is a deaf-mute." The German looks at Abram with disgust and shoves him back into the crowd. Thank heaven!

Slowly I make my way toward Abram, still holding on to my little companion. Abram sees me now. He pushes toward me with all his strength and grabs my free hand. His eyes shine with joy. We press each other's hands. How wonderful to see a friend.

The sun is slowly disappearing, giving way to the darkness of the evening. I keep on thinking of Mama, the pain she must be suffering.

It was early morning when Saba and I left home on a small errand, and now it is evening. Her heart must be breaking. With Jews shot daily, people being taken to the Gestapo to be tortured . . . How horrible it must be, waiting in despair, not knowing where her child is, not knowing if I am alive or dead.

Stop and go, pushed, kicked, we are led to the railroad station. Gunshots cut through the air. People groan, cry, pray. Suddenly we hear: "Halt! All men to the right! Women and children to the left!"

We all seem to be frozen. "Move! Move! Faster! Faster!" shout the Germans, pulling men to the right, cursing and hitting them.

From all directions voices call names, addresses. "Tell my family. Give them my love. Tell them not to worry!" Children crying, women screaming, men shouting frantic messages: All mix together in a loud roar of terror, anger, pain.

I feel my little friend's nails digging into my flesh. I look at him. His pale face is a frozen mask of horror. Maybe it is the reflection of my own face. I wish I could smile to calm him. How do you smile in this madness? I pull him and Abram close to me.

The Germans separate all the men from the women and children. Surrounded by the soldiers, rifles pointed at them, they move forward. The women and children remain motionless. Our bewildered eyes follow the men as they disappear from sight. We are free to go home.

In painful silence, shocked, trembling, Abram and I walk our little companion home.

The streets are covered in darkness. Deserted. It is long past the hour of curfew for the Jews. From many doorways worried, frightened eyes stare, searching in the dark for familiar faces. Outcries of joy and screams of despair fill the night. Elation on seeing a loved one alive and safe; grief, agony on receiving the tragic news: Your husband, your father, your son are not coming home. . . .

A woman runs toward our little friend with outstretched arms. He runs into her waiting embrace.

Good-bye, my little comrade of the horror caravan.

I realize then that I never asked him his name. His pale face, his horrified eyes will always remain with me.

Abram and I run now. Home, to see our families again. To feel their loving arms again. To feel safe again.

In front of the apartment house, they are waiting. Mama, her face ashen, her eyes swollen from crying. My little brothers, Motele, Laibele, Moishele. Saba is also with them. Thank heaven!

Abram's parents, brother, sister stand in the

doorway. All our neighbors are waiting. I see Mrs. Avner. My heart stops. How do I tell her? How do I tell her?

"They are coming! They are coming!" I hear Motele shout with joy. In seconds Mama's arms are around me. I feel her hot tears on my face. They blend with my own tears as I hear her whisper, "I thought I lost you. I thought I lost you."

Mrs. Avner never sees her husband again. The men of our caravan of horror are sent to labor camps or shot.

5

May 1940. The gates of the ghetto in Lodz are shut tight. One hundred eighty thousand Jewish men, women, and children are herded together inside a barbed-wire cage. Unemployment, hunger, disease: They come together and spread their pain and misery. The Nazis order all machinery surrendered to them. No more factories. No more jobs.

Mothers look helpless, with tears in their eyes at the faces of their hungry children. Fathers, angry and frustrated, spend their days looking for work, only to find all doors closed to them. Lost, bewildered children move about, wondering what to do with all their free time.

Vacation is long over, but no schools are open for the children of the ghetto. They play a new game—escape from the Germans. They form two groups, Jews and Germans. The idea is not to get caught by the Germans trying to find and kill the Jews. . . .

the cage

A *Judenrat*, a Jewish council appointed by the Nazis and watched over by them, governs the ghetto. Despair turns the people against them.

An outcry, "March to the Judenrat," reaches the homes. It spreads swiftly over the ghetto and brings thousands of people out of their crowded rooms into the lines of a march for life.

Mama, Motele, Laibele, Moishele, and I join the march. Many others join on our way. "We want work!" people shout. "We want jobs for our mothers and fathers! We want food for our hungry children! We want bread! We want to live!" Voices of young and old form one desperate outcry.

We reach our destination, the Judenrat. The marchers grow louder and angrier. "Schools, bread, jobs," they chant in one voice. After hours of shouting, the door to the Judenrat office is finally opened. The people ask for a delegation to present the issues to the Judenrat and try to find a way to ease the problems.

The march for life does bring results: kitchens to supply soup and bread, hospitals, schools, factories. In a short time the ghetto has its own well-organized government under the dictatorship of Chaim Rumkowski, a man hungry for power and wealth.

But the soup kitchens, schools, and hospitals do not last very long. Again hunger and disease take over and spread in the crowded ghetto. Tuberculosis and dysentery hit every home and spread like wildfire, taking hundreds of lives daily.

My little brother Laibele contracts tuberculosis. Confined to his bed, he stays alone all day, waiting for the moment when the door will finally open and Mama, Motele, Moishele, and I return home from a long day in the tailor shops, bringing him love and some soup that we all saved for him from our rations at work.

Now that the Nazis have taken away our factory, we work at several shops. I work at the same shop as Mama. Together we sew German military coats all day long. My back bends over from the weight of the heavy coats. My fingers bleed from the stabbing and piercing of the sharp needles. My body aches. I wish I could rest for a while, just a little while. The needle slips slowly out from my young, inexperienced fingers and rests angrily in the coat on my lap.

Do not stop now, says the sharp needle. *Keep going. Hold me tighter. Work. Work. Work. If you want to live, work. Work.* Startled, I put my fingers tighter around the needle and work.

I feel anger rising within me, a small voice trying to get out and shout to all those tired souls around me, *Look at us, look at us. Look at what we are sewing: coats for Germans to wear at the front, to keep them warm so they stay healthy and kill, kill, kill!* But the angry voice within me does not reach my lips. It remains, shouting, inside of me.

I look at Mama, working next to me. Her face pale and sad, her tears flowing silently over her sunken cheeks bring a stabbing pain to my heart. I feel her anguish. It is Laibele she is crying for, the sweet, gentle child she has to leave, sick, cold, and lonely, at home.

I still hear the doctor's voice: *I am so sorry. I wish I could do something for him. I wish I could help. He has tuberculosis. He needs good food, fresh air, better living conditions, medicine. Maybe then he would have a chance.*

But my little brother has no chance. He is only thirteen. He lies in his bed all day long, dreaming of Mama's warm touch, her smile.

It is cold at home. There is no coal or wood left to keep the house warm. The wooden partition used to separate the kitchen from the bedroom has long since been taken apart and used for firewood. Even some of the furniture has been burned.

Laibele looks all day at the frost-covered windows and the pretty, icy flowers Mother Nature paints. He marvels at their beauty while dreaming of a better tomorrow.

He is such a sensitive child. We have to force him to take an extra share of bread, a little more soup. He pleads, "Don't give me your food. You will all get sick. It will not help me get well."

Mama touches his face and whispers softly, "You will get well. This nightmare will end soon. You will get well again."

He wants so much to believe those words. He wants so much to live. He cuddles close to Mama and whispers, "I love you so very much." He wipes the tears from Mama's cheeks.

Many evenings I sit at the edge of his bed. I tell him what is happening in our barbed-wire cage, what life is like outside his room, at the shop, at our secret study groups. "Laibele," I

the cage

say, "there are no more schools for us here. But we cannot let the Nazis destroy our minds. Some of us have formed secret study groups. If we have no teachers, we will teach one another."

He listens with interest to my every word. His eyes shine. I speak to him of a tomorrow that is coming for all of us. "This day will come, my darling brother. You'll see, you'll see. We'll walk out of this cage, free to build a new life, a new world. No more hunger. Freedom, happiness. A world of brotherhood. A world of love and peace."

He takes my hand in his, looks into my eyes, searching for the answer, and whispers, "Will I live to see that day? Do I have a chance?"

I hold him tightly, kiss his light brown hair, and, trying to sound strong, positive, I say, "You will live. We will all survive."

Now I look at Mama, and I wish I could find words to ease her pain. She wants so much to be with her sick child, to hold him, to comfort him.

The harsh, metallic shrieking of the sewing machines fills the air. I look at the human skeletons bending over the machines, pushing the pedals with their last bit of strength. Is there a tomorrow for them? Is there a tomorrow for me?

Suddenly screams fill the crowded room. People run, their eyes filled with terror and despair. I run, too.

On the floor I see stretched out, hardly breathing, a young man. His eyes are closed, his face ashen, his hands pressed against his heart. From his lips blood silently flows over his bony chin and forms one big black spot on the wooden floor.

I look with horror at the blood of his dying lungs, leaving his body. His eyes flash a last, desperate cry for help. Then they close forever.

His body is removed. The dark, ugly spot formed by the blood of his lungs remains. It says to me, *This is what is waiting for you. For your mother. For your brothers.* I cover my mouth to hold back my screams. I run to Mama's arms.

The shrieking and crying of the sewing machines fill the air again.

6

September 1942. The ghetto walls are closing in. Terror and panic fill every home. Nazis are inside the ghetto, taking away the sick, the old, and the children.

The streets are deserted. The deadly silence is broken by the sound of the Nazis' marching and their commands: "Jews, out! Jews, out!" Sudden horrified cries let us know that the messengers of death are here.

Mama stands near Laibele's bed, caressing with trembling hands his delicate, pale face. His frightened eyes search Mama's face, looking for an answer: How can he be saved from the Nazis? They want to take him from us. "There are hospitals, better places for the sick and the old," they say.

"They will not take you, my child. They will not take you," Mama says with determination. "Motele," she calls frantically, "open the trap-door to the cellar! Rifkele, get blankets! Moishele, bring pillows! We are hiding Laibele.

The Nazis will not get him!"

Motele opens the trapdoor to the cellar, which is used for storage. We throw the blankets and pillows on the clay floor. Mama places Laibele gently on the pillows and closes the cellar door. We cover the trapdoor with a rug and put a table and chairs over it.

I look at Mama. The horror in her eyes, the ash-gray color of her face fill me with panic. "Please, Mama," I beg, "hide with Laibele in the cellar. You look sick. Please don't go out now."

Motele and Moishele take her by the hand. "Please, Mama, stay here with Laibele."

"No, my children. I must go outside with you. Maybe they won't search the house if they see a family walking together. They don't know we have a sick child. Maybe Laibele will have a chance. . . ." She whispers a silent prayer.

"Jews, out! Everyone, out! Line up! Faster! Faster!" German commands mix with the whistling sound of their whips.

Scared and trembling, people come out from all the apartments. Some older people are dragged by the Nazis.

We line up together, Mama, Motele,

Moishele, and I. I press Mama's hand. I feel her body trembling, see her fearful eyes fixed on the door of the house.

I stare at Mama's worn, tired face. The lovely, gentle face has lost all trace of liveliness. Her pretty blue eyes are red and swollen from sleepless nights and endless tears; her dark hair is woven with gray now. I want to scream, scream, scream.

Our line is moving forward. "Right. Left. Right. Left. Left," command the Nazis. How easy it is for them to separate families. "Faster, Jews! You, old man, to the left! You, you, you, right!"

Motele and Moishele are in front of Mama. The Nazi looks closely at them. I hold my breath. Motele is fifteen, Moishele only eleven. They hold their heads high, trying to look older. "To the right," he says after a moment— or was it a lifetime? They are safe.

Mama is before me. Her eyes are glued to the house. The Nazis are searching our apartment.

"What work do you do?" asks the Nazi. She does not answer; she cannot speak. She pulls out her workman's card. She is head instructor at a tailor shop. She is an excellent worker and is needed, says the card.

He gives her a cold stare. "You can't work; you are sick. Left!" He pushes her aside.

We run after her. She holds us for a split second—the last time.

The soldiers pull us back. Our screams don't bother them. They push her into the waiting wagon. We run toward the wagon, pleading, begging. "Please, let her go. She is a young woman. She is not sick!"

Mama stretches her loving arms toward us. Motele is standing near the wagon, calling, "Mama, jump. Mama, jump!"

She is trying to jump into Motele's arms, but the two steel hands of a ghetto policeman hold her back. Motele tries to pull her away from the policeman, pull her off the wagon. The policeman kicks him to the ground and speeds up the wagon.

I hear Mama's agonizing scream, and the wagon disappears from sight. Moishele and I help Motele up. He is bleeding. I wipe the blood with my sleeve. We stare at one another in shock—three bewildered kids in the middle of an empty world.

"Laibele, is he safe?" I hear Moishele's voice. We run to the house. The table and chairs are in the same place over the trapdoor. They did not find the cellar. We pull the trapdoor open: Laibele is safe.

How do you tell a sick child that he has no mother? How do you tell it to yourself? I am sixteen, and I feel so lost and helpless.

We do not have to say anything to Laibele. He reads it in our faces. His eyes grow bigger and bigger; his mouth twists in pain. He whispers, "No. No."

I put my arms around him, pressing him tightly to me. "Cry, darling, cry."

With his hot tears pouring over my face, I know I am no longer a sixteen-year-old girl. I am a mother now.

For days the four of us hardly eat or sleep. We huddle together on Mama's bed and cry.

Outside the days are warm and sunny. I look at the sky and wonder, How can the sun still shine?

7

Slowly life in the ghetto begins again. With the help of friends, I manage to get a job that I can do from the house: From a rug factory I receive scraps of fabric, which I braid and roll into large rolls to be used in the making of rugs for the Germans.

As a "home-worker," I lose the right to the daily soup given at the factory. But I get to stay home with Laibele and care for him.

Motele and Moishele save their portions of soup until they come home at five. We all share their soup for our dinner.

Laibele's condition worsens, and the gall-stones that I developed two years ago cause painful attacks—with Mama's love and care, the pain was easier to endure—but we try to comfort each other with our devotion.

My legs swell up more and more, but there is nothing I can do about it. I try to keep my brothers from noticing it. They cannot help; why make them worry?

the cage

One morning, as I get out of my bed, my legs buckle. I lose my balance and fall back against the bed. I feel silly and try to smile. Startled, Laibele looks at me from across the room. But, seeing my embarrassed smile, he makes a joke of it: "Well, well, my sister is drunk today. I bet you can't walk a straight line from your bed to mine."

"Oh, so you are a wise guy now."

I stand up, but my legs give way again, and I fall to the floor. We stop smiling. I try to hide my fear. "Well, you win. I am drunk."

"You must be very tired. You have to rest a little more today." Laibele's eyes are filled with worry.

I pull myself up and get back to bed. Several hours later I try again and fall again. My feet refuse to hold me up. Day after day, I keep trying; day after day, I keep falling.

Motele tries to get a doctor to come to the house. No luck. Our neighbor, Mrs. Avner, shriveled and hardly holding herself up, looks in on us daily. Her son-in-law, Moishe, spends the evenings with us, trying to keep up our spirits.

It is heartbreaking to see the fear in

Laibele's eyes. Now that I am his mother, will he lose me, too?

"Rifkele, please eat my bread. It will help you get stronger," he pleads. I refuse; he gets angry with me. But he finally gives in and eats his meager portion of bread.

One evening, Moishele, his blue eyes shining, bends over my bed, his hands hidden behind his back. "Close your eyes and open your mouth."

"What are you up to?" I ask.

"Come on, listen to him," Motele and Laibele join in. "Open your mouth, close your eyes. Trust us."

They are excited and very mysterious.

"All right, I'll play your game." I open my mouth slightly.

Moishele slips something soft through my lips. "Bite into it," he urges. "Come on, bite into it."

Slowly, cautiously I bite into the plump, soft object. A burst of sweet, tangy juice fills my mouth suddenly with a delightful, long-forgotten taste. Is it real? Is it possible? A tangerine? A real tangerine in the ghetto? In our home? In my mouth?

the cage

I open my eyes. Motele's joyous smile, his proud look tell me it is real. Holding the tangerine in his hand, Moishele says, "We traded our bread for it at the black market. This will help you get well. You'll see, you'll see."

Tears choke me. My darling brothers, they gave up their bread—they will go hungry a whole week—for one tangerine. They are waiting for a miracle from one tangerine. I should be angry at them, but they are my miracle. Their devotion is the greatest wonder in this cage.

My tears finally break loose. "I love you all so much." I take the tangerine, break it into sections, put it on a plate. "I will not eat it alone. We'll give Laibele half—he is sick—and we'll share the rest. We'll have a party."

"But it's for you, to make you well," they protest.

I push the plate aside. "We'll share, or I will not eat. I mean it." We share. I swallow the sweet pieces of the fruit slowly, savoring each drop of the delicious nectar, my heart bursting with love for those three beautiful kids, my kids.

I must get well. I must get well.

8

"I will find a doctor for you. I will," our neighbor, Moishe, says one day, his voice determined and angry. "You cannot just stay in bed and rot. I won't allow it."

I smile sadly. "Moishe, Moishe, no wonder they call you *meshuggener* Moishe. You *are* crazy. Where will you find a doctor to look at me? There are very few doctors in the ghetto, and they are too busy to come to the house."

"Don't you call me meshugge! I am not crazy. I'll find a doctor. You'll see. I'll show them all what a meshuggener Moishe can do."

I look at him closely. He is in his thirties, medium height, skinny, pale. With his angry, burning eyes, his clenched fists, he looks like a madman about to fight the world.

For a whole week, he does not show up at our house. I wonder if I hurt his feelings. What right do I have to call him crazy? Maybe I am the one who is crazy, waiting for a better tomorrow that may never come for us. . . .

the cage

Then, one morning, he comes, radiant, excited, shouting, "Get dressed! I am taking you to see a doctor. My Simcia will stay with Laibele. Hurry! Hurry! Let's go."

I stare at him. "I cannot walk. How will I get to the doctor?"

"You just get ready and don't ask stupid questions. I am the meshuggener here, remember?"

As soon as I am dressed, he picks me up in his arms and carries me out the door into the street. The cool, fresh air feels so invigorating and clean. It has been weeks since I felt fresh air caressing my face, a breeze gently playing with my hair.

I feel awkward and embarrassed being carried through the street like a small child. "Moishe, how far are we going? I feel so clumsy and silly. I am too big and too heavy to be carried like a baby. People are staring at us, Moishe."

"So what? Besides, people in the ghetto are not surprised at anything anymore. You are not the only one who cannot walk."

"You know, Moishe, you do have the right nickname. And I am glad you are my friend."

He smiles, pleased with himself.

"So where is the doctor's office, Moishe, my friend?"

"Not too far. Only a little way more. On Lutomierska Street."

"Lutomierska!" I cry out. "You mean on the other side of the ghetto bridge? You are going to carry me all the way there? You can't carry me that far! It's five blocks to the bridge, two long flights of stairs to the overpass, two flights down to the other side of the ghetto, two more blocks to the doctor's office. Who do you think you are, Samson? What happens if the guard at the bridge is bored today and he feels like having some fun and starts shooting at us to amuse himself? Can you run with me in your arms? Let's go back, Moishe. You cannot make it over the bridge." I rattle on, frantic.

"Now, you stop this and be still. You have a short memory, Rifkele. You told me I have the right nickname, remember? A meshuggener can do anything, so stop your blabbering, put your arms around my neck, and be still. You'll make it easier on both of us."

I put my arms around his neck, put my head on his shoulder, and whisper softly, "May you be blessed with the strength of Samson today."

We make it across the bridge safely. The guard does not pay any attention to us. He stands in his booth playing with his rifle. Moishe's heavy breathing tells me that his strength is giving out, but he keeps on going, taking only short rests. He carries me up three flights to the doctor's office and puts me down on a chair with a triumphant look. "We made it, see? See what a meshuggener can do?"

The small room is crowded with people, most of whom look more like human skeletons than men and women. I feel healthy looking at them. If it were not for the problem with my legs . . .

After a long wait, our turn comes. The doctor, a man in his fifties, looking worn, examines me carefully, asking very few questions. I keep my eyes glued to his face, trying to read the verdict in his expression. Is there hope for me? But all I see in his face is frustration, helplessness, pity.

"What is wrong with her, doctor?" Moishe can't stand the suspense any longer. "Can you help her? Can you do something for her?"

Avoiding my eyes, the doctor looks at Moishe sadly. "I wish I could. I wish I could. I know her problem—malnutrition, vitamin deficiency, loss of calcium in her bones—but the cure I cannot supply. I wish I could help her, and all the others. . . ."

I feel sorry for the helpless doctor. I feel sorry for Moishe and his wasted effort. I feel sorry for myself.

9

I stay in bed day after day, making braids for rugs. Motele receives permission to pick up the material for me from the rug factory, so I can work in bed.

Laibele's sense of humor, his strong will to live, his wisdom keep up my morale. "Hey, big sister, what happened to your smile? Is it still sleeping? Knock, knock, Mr. Smile. It is morning. Wake up!" he calls. "Mr. Smile, if you are lost, we'll have to search for you, so come on, don't play hard to find. I know you are only hiding. I am waiting." He makes funny faces at me until he sees a smile on my face.

We play games, tell stories, crack jokes. Our favorite game is What If? "What if the war came to an end today, Laibele? What would be the first thing you would do?"

"I would get a huge loaf of bread and eat, eat, eat until I could eat no more and I would never feel hungry again."

We speak about Mama and the day when

she will return to us, about our sisters, Mala and Chanele, and our brother Yankele. We wonder where they are, what life is like for them in a distant, strange land, away from their loved ones. "They must be so lonely, and I am sure they are also wondering what is happening to us, Laibele. I have an idea! I'll write them daily letters and tell them about our life in the ghetto."

"You are so silly, Rifkele. You know there is no mail going out or coming into the ghetto, so why write?"

"Well, if the war ends tomorrow and they come home, we will not have to tell them anything. We will just give them their mail, and it will answer all their questions."

In the back of my mind, I have a different thought: What if we do not survive to answer their questions? The letters will tell them our story.

I write my first letter that day to my sisters and brother far away from home.

"I think of Mama often. I miss her so much," Laibele says one day. "I know when she returns she will be disappointed and angry because we have stopped studying. Maybe you should start teaching me again, and Motele and Moishele. You always wanted to be a teacher. Start with us. We have some books. You will be the teacher, we will be the students, and we'll have our own private school." His eyes glow with excitement; his pale face has a touch of color. We must be ready for Mama's return, for the tomorrow that is coming!

The four of us talk it over that same evening. Laibele is right: Mama will be hurt if we do not continue our study of history, Jewish literature. The stories of Sholem Aleichem, the poems and stories of I. L. Peretz, Reisen, Kulbak will become part of our daily routine.

"I love the way you tell the adventures of Sholem Aleichem's Motel and his brother Elie. They make me laugh," says Moishele.

I put my arms around him. "It is good to hear you laugh, my dear brother. Sholem Aleichem said, 'Laughter is good for your health.' If laughter is such good medicine, let's laugh, laugh, laugh. Maybe it will even make us well. . . ."

But we need much more than laughter to make us well. It does not cure tuberculosis or put calcium back into my bones.

One evening, looking nervous and excited, Motele hands me a small bottle. "Rifkele, before you get angry at us, please listen. This bottle contains vitamins that will make your bones strong again. They are called Vigantol. We waited a long time for them to be smuggled into the ghetto. We were lucky; they are impossible to get. Please don't be mad. We love you. We need you."

I stare at the little bottle in my hand for a while. "How did you pay for it, Motele? Look at me. How did you pay for it?"

"Well," he stammers, "we could not ask your permission. You would have said no. But we talked it over," he adds quickly. "We all agreed. We sold our bread ration for the week. It will be all right, you'll see, you'll see."

Laibele and Moishe echo, "It will be all right, Rifkele. Please don't be mad. Please."

"This better make me well, you crazy kids." I try to sound tough, taking the dropper filled with vitamins. Raising it high, I say, "L'chaim. L'chaim. To life."

"L'chaim. L'chaim," they reply in one happy voice.

the cage

I show improvement. The selling of our bread for vitamins is repeated. Holding on to the walls and furniture, I start to move about in the house.

10

One day a social worker from the ghetto Child Welfare Department comes to see us. She looks around the house and asks questions while carefully studying each of us. Finally, with warmth and compassion in her voice, she states the reason for her visit: It has been reported that we, four young children, live alone, without adult supervision.

"We cannot allow this to continue and must find proper homes for all of you. We have many families who lost their children. They will be happy to have a child in their home to fill the emptiness in their hearts. We will even find a home for Laibele." She speaks softly, slowly, as if trying to lessen the horrible blow of her words.

I look at her gentle face, her kind eyes, her slight build and wonder how this fragile-looking woman has the strength to utter such words. How can she carry the burden of separating a family?

I look at Laibele, and Mama's pleading eyes are before me. I hear a voice within me crying, *A mother does not give up her children! A mother does not give up her children!*

I look at her and the anger rises in my voice: "Don't try to break our hearts again. You will not separate us. Please leave us alone!"

She does not leave us alone. She comes again and again, bringing vitamins for me, an egg for Laibele, bread for all of us. And always she brings the same horrible word from her superiors: adoption. I beg her to forget us, to let us have what little happiness we have. Finally I refuse to let her in.

"Rifkele, you know you cannot fight them much longer. We are helpless against them. They will have their way in the end," says Motele.

I am not sure anymore. Am I right to fight adoption? Maybe they would be better off, find good homes, be happy. Is it wrong to want to hold our family together? Does my love for them give me the right to decide what is best for them? Do I know what is best for them?

One day a special messenger brings a summons, ordering each of us to appear at the

Child Welfare Department. We have no choice but to go.

Laibele stays home. His body is consumed by tuberculosis, but his mind is clear and sharp. He wishes us luck, following us sadly with his eyes.

We walk, Motele, Moishele, and I, holding hands, without saying a word. My weak legs move very slowly.

In the Child Welfare Department, we are taken to separate rooms. I wait, my heart pounding violently, my eyes fixed on the door. It opens, and a young woman walks in. I know who she is: Miss Wolkowna, the head of the Child Welfare Department. She looks silently at me. I study her face, calm and serious. Does this mean her decision is made? Will she listen to me?

"I suppose you know what I called you about. Your case has been pointed out to me, and I wanted to meet you. You look to me intelligent enough to understand we mean well, we want to help you. We know what is best for you and your brothers. We will find good homes for Motele and Moishele. I am willing to adopt you. I know more about you than you think."

She pauses for a moment. "And Laibele will go to a home for children."

"Home for children," I repeat with a trembling voice. "That means he will be with the first new victims for the Nazi transports! Is that why Mama sacrificed her life? So Laibele should be sent to a home to wait for deportation? Is that what you are asking me to do? Send him willingly to his death?

"Good homes for my brothers! A good home for me! Do you think a little more bread, an extra piece of meat will take the place of brotherly love, give us the warmth of our home? Our house is empty without Mama, but our hearts are not. The love for one another that she planted there will always be with us. We can only be happy together. Please do not destroy us! Leave us alone. Please. . . ."

My tears give way, pour freely over my face. She puts her hand on my head. I see the tears in her eyes. With quivering lips, she places a soft kiss on my hair. Without saying a word, she leaves the room.

I wait outside for the boys. Motele comes out first, his eyes burning with anger. Then Moishele, his face pale, frightened. He takes my hand in his, holds it tightly. "I do not want to leave our home. Do you think they can force me?"

Motele looks at me. We all know that we cannot stop them. We walk in silence for a while. Then Motele breaks the silence. "I told them we did not come for help. All we want is to be left alone! Is that too much to ask? I will not leave, no matter what they do!"

Laibele has waited in fearful anticipation for our return. He looks carefully at each of us, trying to read the verdict from our faces. Then a smile covers his delicate face. "I knew we would not give up," he says with pride.

We live in a state of waiting and wondering. Are these our last days together? Is there a tomorrow for us? The agony is on our faces, but we do not speak about it. There is nothing left to say.

Every knock at our door makes our hearts stop beating. Are they coming for us?

And then one day I am called into the Child Welfare Department alone. Slowly I open the door to the same office as before.

The social worker is at her desk. She runs

toward me and throws her arms around me, shouting with joy, "Good news, my child! Good news!"

I look at her, dazed. She pulls me over to her desk and points at some papers. "You know what these papers are?" Her voice is jubilant, elated. "They are your adoption papers!"

I see my whole world crumble before me.

"Oh, no!" she says quickly, putting her arms around me to hold me up. "It is not what you think. We had a special session about your case. We decided to make an exception to our rules, seeing the love and devotion you have for one another. We feel that you all deserve to keep what you have. You are going to be the only sixteen-year-old to be a legal guardian of younger children. That means you are adopting your own brothers! At the same time—I must point this out to you before you sign—you are losing the rights of a child. Today you become an adult."

For a moment I just stand there, over-whelmed. It has happened. Our dream has come true! We are not being separated! We have one another! We have our home! We are still a family!

I grab her hands, hug them tightly, whispering, "Oh, thank you! Oh, thank you!"

That day, for the first time in weeks, we breathe freely. The four of us cuddle together on Laibele's bed, full of joy, forgetting for the moment that we are still in the ghetto cage.

11

Motele and Moishele make their daily trip to work. Their school is the tailor shop; their books, the sewing machine; their lesson, the making of German military uniforms.

I look at their tired blue eyes and try to recall their smiles. The gleam in Moishele's eyes, always full of mischief—it was so long, long ago.

I look at Motele. He looks much older than his fifteen years. His eyes are the eyes of an old man who has seen all the misery of life but will not give up fighting for a better tomorrow. His voice is strong, mature, serious.

I wonder at the changes that make us all. We are so old.

I spend many hours sitting on Laibele's bed, reading to him, talking, playing games.

"I wonder if the free world, outside our cage, is still the same, Riva. Do people outside the ghetto live a normal life? Do they go to schools, to shows? Do they ever feel hungry?

Riva, do you think—is it possible?—that the great, big world has forgotten about us? Does anybody care? Sometimes I wonder, Riva."

I put my fingers on his mouth. Such doubt . . . and from him. "Laibele, don't you start with such silly thoughts. You are the strongest among us. You keep up the morale in this house. I do not want to hear such words. Not from your lips. I am sure the world outside the cage remembers us. They will come to our rescue soon, very soon."

A faint grin covers his tired face. "From your mouth to God's ears—if God has not forgotten us."

I look at my sweet little brother, slowly fading away, and I, too, wonder. . . .

A sudden knock at the door echoes through the house, startling both of us. We hold our breath and wait. I left the door unlocked for Mrs. Avner to come in, but she would not knock. We hold hands, silently praying.

From Laibele's bed the front door is out of sight, but we can hear it being opened. Footsteps. Someone is slowly moving about in the kitchen. My heart stops. Is this the end for us? Are the Nazis searching for the sick again?

the cage

What do I do with Laibele? I cannot hide him now. Our cellar is in the kitchen. I must not panic. Sit still. Wait. Hope.

A mournful lament breaks the deadly silence, fills the house with its grief, sends chills down my spine. "There is no one left of my family! There is no one left of my friends! They are all gone! All gone!"

There is something familiar about that voice. I make my way slowly toward the kitchen door. I hear the voice again, but now it is the hoarse whisper of a broken man. "They are all gone, all dead."

My God. It is Shmulek's voice. Our neighbor. Our friend. I stop short. It can't be. He left a year ago, as a volunteer for a labor camp. They assured him that he was helping his family, but they were all deported a short while after he left: his mother, his brothers, his sisters. They are all gone. He made his sacrifice, but it did not help them survive.

It cannot be Shmulek. No one ever returns from a labor camp. Cautiously, slowly, I peek through the kitchen door. I see the figure of a man, his head bowed, his feet dragging heavily toward the door. He is leaving.

I stare at the black, curly hair, the broad shoulders. It *is* Shmulek! I want to run to him but stay frozen. I want to call out to him but stay speechless, choked up, paralyzed. From deep inside of me an agonizing cry finally tears out. "Shmulek! We are still here! Shmulek! We are still alive."

He turns toward me. He stares at my face. He touches my hair, my eyes. "Riva . . . Riva . . . You are real? You are alive? It is not a dream? I thought there was no one left anymore."

We fall into each other's arms.

12

"I am sure you are all eager to hear what I am doing here. I am searching for my family. I was so sure that they were all here, waiting for me, for the day that I would come home. . . ." He stops, takes a deep breath, swallows hard. The four of us wait silently.

"In the labor camp there were Jews and non-Jews from ghettos and prisons. They were sent there to build good roads for the German army to travel on. We worked very, very hard. The days were long and lonely. I felt that the hunger, the hard work, the hardship was all worthwhile. I was helping my family to survive. The commandant kept announcing that our hard work helped the people we left behind. 'The harder you work here, the more food your family receives!' And we believed him.

"I became a model slave laborer, worked with all my strength. Last night five of us were suddenly called to the commandant. We were all scared. 'You are being sent back to the ghetto

Lodz, to your families. This is your reward for being such good workers.'

"We stood there, frozen. No one was ever sent back to the ghetto. Was this some kind of excuse to keep us calm before they executed us?

"In front of the commandant's office there was a horse and wagon ready and waiting. Three guards sat on the wagon, rifles pointed at us. 'Get into the wagon fast, before I change my mind!' the commandant ordered.

"We got into the wagon, wondering all along the way where we were really going. To our surprise, they did bring us back here, to the ghetto. They had the ghetto guards open the gates, shove us forward, and close the gates again behind us.

"I ran all the way here. 'I am going home,' I shouted. 'I am going to see my mother, my sisters, my brothers again.' I could feel my mother's arms around me." He swallowed hard again. "Look what I found. All gone. My family is all gone."

Silence. Silence. Such painful silence.

"Tell me," Shmulek says, "tell me about my family. How did they look when they were sent away? Were they healthy? All the men at the labor camp were young, still strong enough to work. There were no women in that camp. They may have camps where women work. Maybe my sisters . . . They are young. But my mother . . . What kind of work can my mother do? Where did they take her? I have nothing without them. Tomorrow I'll ask to be sent back to slave labor. Maybe they will send me to the same camp. Maybe I will find them."

We all feel his agony, his hope.

"Maybe if I had stayed here, if I had not left them alone . . . maybe they would still be here. It is my fault. I signed up for slave labor. I believed what I was told. My family was to get more food, a pension to help them survive. I was so sure that I was helping them. I did it all for—"

"Shmulek!" Motele cuts in sharply. "Shmulek, stop this! You did what you had to do to help your family. For a while they did get a pension, they did receive a little more in their food rations. Your mother missed you. She cried a lot. But she was also very proud of you.

"You left your home to help the people you love. You made a huge sacrifice. You cannot blame yourself. Shmulek, we all know that when they need new people to be sent out of the ghetto, they always find a reason for the new lists. Shmulek"—his voice wavers—"Shmulek, they make new lists every day. Who knows whose name will be next on the list. Who knows what tomorrow will bring."

Moishele puts his arms on Shmulek's shoulders. "We are happy to see you alive, Shmulek. Welcome back. Stay with us."

"Yes, yes, stay with us," Motele and Laibele echo. "Stay here."

I feel myself blush. "Yes, Shmulek has to be part of our family now, but—but he cannot sleep here with us."

All eyes turn toward me. I look at Shmulek, searching for the right words. "Shmulek, I am not sending you away. I only want you to sleep next door at my friend Henry's house. It may sound very silly to you, but I still care what people will say. You are a young man of twenty; I, a young lady of sixteen. They will gossip. Do you understand? I hope you do."

I study his handsome face closely. With his dark eyes, black curly hair, and dark complexion, he looks like a movie star who is playing a part in which he is trying to rescue his loved ones and take them to freedom.

Gently, he takes my hands in his. He looks at me as if seeing me for the first time. A grin slowly covers his face, and there is a twinkle in his eyes. "I understand," he says softly.

"Henry is a very nice young man." I feel more composed now. "We went to school together. When Mrs. Gruber, our landlady, moved to the nicest part of Lodz as a *Volksdeutsche*, his family and two other families all moved in together to Mrs. Gruber's two-room apartment. There were eight of them: Henry, his mother and father, a couple with a small baby, and a very young pair of newly-weds.

"They lived as one large family. Then Henry's mother died of tuberculosis. His father did not last very long afterward. He just faded away. The baby was taken away by the Nazis, and the mother lost her mind. They took her away. The father left on his own for the slave labor camps. He had nothing left.

"The other couple could not stand living in this house anymore. They had all been such close friends. Now Henry has the apartment to himself. I am sure he will be glad to have another human being in that lonely, empty apartment."

Motele goes to call Henry. He comes—a tall, skinny young man of seventeen with earnest, somber eyes—and looks at Shmulek from behind his heavy glasses with sympathy and warmth. They shake hands, exchange greetings, and leave together.

I sit down to write a letter:

> Dear Mama,
> I am not sure that I did right, sending Shmulek, who is all alone now, to the home of a stranger. I know some people feel that the moral codes we grew up with have no meaning anymore. There may not be any tomorrow. . . .
> But I cannot feel that way, even if there is no tomorrow. I still care what people think, and I feel that I have to do what I think is right.
> I miss you so very, very much. I need you. I need your love. When you come home, when

Mala, Chanele, and Yankele come
back home, I do not want any of
you to be ashamed of me.
Your loving daughter,
Your Rifkele

I put the letter in the drawer, together with
all the other letters never to be mailed.

13

A sharp knocking at the door wakes us. We hold our breath. We do not dare make a sound. It could be Nazis searching again for the sick, for children, for the old. The pounding at the door gets stronger. A voice, harsh and angry, calls, "Open up! This is the Jewish police! Open the door, or we'll break it open!"

Motele opens the door. Four policemen rush into the house. They push him aside roughly. "Where is Shmulek Nachtigal? We came to take him back. Now, where are you hiding him? Tell us where he is."

Their angry voices frighten me. What will they do to him if they find him? Why are they searching for him? Does he know something they wanted to keep secret? If he does, he did not say anything to us.

Motele looks at me. Our eyes meet in silent understanding. "Shmulek Nachtigal? He was sent to slave labor a year ago," he says. His voice is calm and composed. "We have not seen him since he was sent out of the ghetto."

My heart is pounding violently. Will they believe him? We have never lied before. Can we get away with it? My mother's words keep running through my head: *Always speak the truth. But if the truth will kill another human being, lie.* We have to lie, for the truth may cost Shmulek his life.

The policemen are searching every corner of the house: the cellar, under each bed, inside each closet. They are pulling everything apart, dumping the clothes all over the floor, like some sort of garbage.

Why are they behaving like this? They, too, are Jews, in the same cage, fighting for survival and the strength to hold out until tomorrow, a tomorrow that will bring us all freedom and dignity. So why do they act as if they were the masters and we were the slaves? We are all slaves here.

"Why are you ruining our clothes and our house? What right do you have to treat your fellow Jews this way? Your lives are not any more protected than ours. Don't fool yourselves. If we survive, you will have to answer for your behavior, remember that."

I raise my voice in spite of my fear. "Shmulek Nachtigal is not in this house. You will not find anybody here except me and my three brothers, so start acting like fellow Jews. We are not the enemy here."

One of the policemen stops for a moment. He looks at me closely, then looks at my brothers as if trying to decide whether he should get angry or ignore my outburst. "Shmulek Nachtigal was sent back to the ghetto last night." He looks straight at me, watching for my reaction. "It was a mistake. The commandant of the camp was drunk. He felt generous and sent five Jews back to the ghetto. Today he is sober, and he wants them back or else. . . .

"The order is to bring them back; they may know too much. If we do not deliver the five men, they will take five of us. You see now, it is them or us.

"We found three men already. The people who live in the Nachtigal apartment now told us that you are Shmulek's only friends. You are the only people left here who know him. So he has to come to you. He has to come here."

"But he never came here." Motele's voice is

sure and unafraid. "If he had, he would still be here."

The policeman turns his head toward Laibele. He shouts: "Is that true? Where did you hide him? You tell me where he is, or I'll take you all in."

Laibele looks frightened, confused. If he tells where Shmulek is, Shmulek may pay with his life. But if he does not, they may take us all.

Motele, outraged, stands in front of the policeman, now shouting: "You leave him alone. Can't you see he's sick? Must you frighten him? If you want to take someone in, take me. You leave my family alone!"

They stand there, both tense, strained, rigid, ready for battle. "All right!" The other policeman breaks the tension. "We'll leave now, but we will return!"

They walk out of the house, slamming the door behind them. Looking toward the door, Motele puts a finger on his lips. We get the message. They are standing behind the door, listening. We all look at him with pride and admiration.

"They are meshugge," Moishele says loudly, "searching for Shmulek here. It has been a year since he was sent to slave labor, and they are looking for him here! They will not find him in this house."

We listen carefully for sounds behind the door. No sounds. After a few minutes, we hear footsteps slowly moving away from our door.

We do not open the door for several hours. We are still not sure if they have really left the building, if it is safe to go to Henry's apartment to warn Shmulek. What if we are being watched? What if they do not believe us and are waiting for a wrong move? We look at one another. What can we do? We hope that Henry and Shmulek heard the commotion during the night and know that Shmulek is in danger. But how do we make sure?

Suddenly Motele picks up an empty bucket for fetching water. The water pump stands in the middle of our yard. To reach it he has to pass Henry's door. He walks slowly, speaking in an angry voice loud enough to be heard behind closed doors: "Riva, you stay in the house while I get water. Don't be scared. The nerve of those policemen, searching for Shmulek here. Did you hear what they said? They will take him back if they find him. If he is back in the ghetto, like they said, I hope he will stay put for a while."

."They may be waiting around in the neighborhood for a few days," I call back. "They said this is the only place he may come to."

Motele fills the bucket with water and walks slowly back. At Henry's door he suddenly turns his ankle and hits his foot against the bucket, kicking it hard against Henry's door, dumping the water all over the hallway. "Now look what I did. How careless of me. Riva, get a mop to wipe the floor, and I'll knock at Henry's door to tell him to be careful when he leaves the apartment. He may get hurt on the wet floor."

He knocks at Henry's door, calling, "It is Motele. We have a problem this morning. I want you to be careful when you step into the hall. It is a mess."

Henry opens the door, looks at the wet floor, looks around him. He gives Motele a pat on the shoulder. "Don't worry, Motele. I will not trip."

"Henry!" I call across the hall. "We have some coffee this morning. Come and have some with us. I'll add a little more water to the pot, and it will be enough for all of us."

"You sure you want to share your coffee with me? I feel guilty taking it away from you."

"Henry, it is only colored water, anyway, and a little more water will not change the color much. So you have nothing to feel guilty about," I say with a smile.

"Well, you've got a point there. I'll come over soon." He comes half an hour later, calmly walking across the hall and closing the door behind him slowly.

"What happened last night?" he asks in a whisper. "We heard policemen knocking at your door. I was going to open the door when I heard the racket, but I remembered the ghetto rule—wait and be sure before you open the door. We both heard whom they were searching for. I had to hold him back with all my strength. He was going to give himself up to protect you all. I begged him to wait and see. We stayed glued to the door, waiting, listening. Finally we heard them leave.

"He is not leaving my house until it is safe. I locked my door from the outside with a padlock. He cannot leave. He will be safe for a while. We'll find a place for him later. I'll speak to my friend Mark. He lives alone, too."

My eyes are full of tears. Henry is risking his life for a stranger he met only last night. I take his hands in mine and press them to my lips. "Thank you, Henry!" Thank you!"

A week later, Henry moves Shmulek to his friend's house. He stays hidden there for several weeks. We all share our food with Shmulek. They finally stop searching for him. He gets a job cleaning the outdoor toilets. He is the horse who pulls the wagon full of human excrement.

14

Winter. Bitter cold, icy winds, heavy snow. The windows are covered with a thick ice coating. A cold wind blows freely through the apartment, pinching our faces with rigid fingers, leaving our cheeks and the tips of our noses colored pink.

Laibele, covered up to his neck with a warm blanket, stares at the frozen windows with a faraway look. "Riva, remember the beautiful poems we learned in school about winter? They sounded so pretty while the house was cheerful and warm. How different they seem now."

"I know how you feel, Laibele. Everything around us looks and feels different now. Nothing has the same meaning anymore. I am not even sure the past was real. Only today is real. But maybe we will learn from today and come out stronger, better people."

A faint smile covers his lips. "My sister, the philosopher. If your philosophy can make you forget about the cold in this house, about your empty stomach, maybe you would like to read me some happy stories."

I cuddle up close to keep him warm and read the adventures of Motel by Sholem Aleichem. Laibele smiles, happily listening to the stories. I touch his head with my lips.

"Riva, remember the story where Motel is in trouble with the other boys? The boys want to hit him, and his neighbor yells at them for trying to hit an orphan. Motel is so happy, and he says, 'I am lucky, for I am an orphan.' Maybe we are a little bit lucky, too, that we are orphans. Maybe God takes special care of orphans."

"Now who is the philosopher?" I say, with a lump in my throat, pulling the blanket closer to his chin. "I wish we had some wood to keep these orphans in here warm."

Then Laibele says, "Remember the oak tree?"

We both look at the ice-covered window, remembering the oak tree.

"I can still hear Mrs. Gruber shouting: 'Next week I am sending some men to cut down the oak tree. I do not want you Jews to enjoy the beauty of my tree!'"

The tree is not outside our window any-more. It was cut down, but not by Mrs. Gruber's men. The ghetto was closed sudden-ly, and she did not get the chance to chop down the tree. It was chopped to pieces by the Jews, whom she wanted to deny the pleasure and beauty of the tree, to keep from freezing. I cried, watching the big, strong tree fall, watch-ing it cut to pieces just as our lives had been.

"Let's sing a happy song to warm our-selves." Laibele's voice scatters my thoughts.

We sing together, the two of us, remember-ing all those who used to sing with us, watch-ing our warm breath dancing like little white clouds around our heads.

Motele looks distraught this evening. He moves restlessly about the house, biting his lips, clenching his fists.

"Motele, you're moving around like an ani-mal ready to split open the iron bars of his cage. I wish you could free us with your bare hands, but you cannot."

He turns his head and stares at the ice-coat-ed windows. "I must get some wood. Look at that heavy layer of ice and snow on the window.

82

You and Laibele stay all day in this icebox. You will both get pneumonia in here. I must get something to warm up this apartment."

"There is nothing left in here to use for firewood," Moishele says, looking around the half-empty rooms. "We burned most of our furniture already."

Motele, a determined, desperate glow in his eyes, silently watches the warm vapors of Moishele's breath disappear in the cold air.

"Why don't you all go to bed?" Laibele calls. "It is much warmer under the blanket. It is late already. Let's go to sleep, and maybe happy dreams will come during the night and bring warmth and peace to our hearts. Maybe . . ."

We follow his advice. At least it will be warmer in bed.

The squeak of our front door being slowly opened wakes me. I open my eyes. In the darkness of the room I see the shadow of a person carrying a bundle in his arms and making his way into the house.

"Who is it?" I whisper, horrified.

"Sha. Sha. Sha, Riva. It is I." I hear Motele's voice. "I got some wood. It will keep us warm for a few days. Some of the men took apart an empty shed. They said if I helped by standing guard, I'd get some of the wood. Riva, no one must know where the wood came from. If we are caught, we are all in trouble."

"You know what the punishment is for stealing wood. Why did you risk your life?" I whisper hoarsely.

"I had to do it. They may call it stealing. I call it helping my family survive. Every day counts. Remember, no matter what happens, you do not know anything about this wood. Promise."

"I promise," I say, angry and proud at the same time.

For several days the colorful flames of the burning wood dance cheerfully in our stove and warm the apartment, brining a glow to our pale cheeks. Laibele and Moishele hold their hands over the sparkling flames, never asking where the wood came from. They know not to ask questions.

I feel panic every time there is a knock at our door. Is it the police? Still, I hope they will not find out. Only a few pieces of wood are left, and soon there will be no trace of the crime.

the cage

Not a trace. One more warm day and the evidence will be gone. We keep the pieces of wood hidden like precious jewels. One more day, and we will be safe.

But the pounding at the door that evening tells us our luck has just run out. The door tears open. Two ghetto policemen burst in, shouting: "Where is the wood that you stole? Who helped you take the shed apart? Tell us whose idea it was, and you'll get off easy!"

They search every corner of the house. They rip apart the closets, pull the bedding off the beds, search under the mattresses. They stop at Laibele's bed, look at each other for a moment, and then reach under his mattress. They pull out a piece of wood. Victorious smiles cover their faces. They have won. They have found the evidence.

All the time they were searching, I felt Motele's eyes piercing me, reminding me. *You promised. You do not know anything. You promised.*

"Who is the oldest here?" one of the policemen asks while taking notes.

"I am the oldest and the legal guardian of my brothers." My voice is shaking. I feel myself shiver.

"Well, we'll take you in, then, and that boy over there." He points to Motele, whose ashen face reveals his rage.

"You two come with us!" He takes me by the arm.

"Leave her alone!" Motele shouts. "Can't you see that she is sick? Look at her swollen legs. She can hardly move about. How could she have carried wood? She had nothing to do with this!"

The policeman looks at me for the first time with pity in his eyes. He shrugs his shoulders and turns to Motele. "Tell us who the leader was. How many were you? Give us their names, and we'll let you go free!"

"I was all alone. No one helped me. I saw the wood on the ground, and I took it home. My sister and my little brother are both sick. They work at home. They freeze all day. The few pieces of wood made them a little bit warmer. Have a heart, leave us alone. Please. Please."

Motele's voice is strong and firm. He will not involve anybody else. The policemen look at each of us, then turn to each other. Silently we wait.

"Sorry. We are really sorry. We have to take Riva in. She is the oldest. And Motele has to come, too, since he took the wood."

"No! No! You will not take my sister!" Moishele steps forward. "She is sick. I will go in her place!"

The policemen stare at each other. I watch their faces. They hold our lives in their hands. Slowly they turn toward me. "We'll let you all stay home today, but Motele will have to report to the police station tomorrow. He took the wood; he is going to be punished. It all depends on the judge."

We sleep very little that night. What will they do to Motele? Some people are sent to labor camps for stealing. But he is only a young boy. Will the judge have a heart? Will he feel for us? We whisper our silent prayers.

Moishele insists on going in with his brother to give him moral support. Laibele and I stay home, counting the hours until they return. The day drags on without end. Horrible thoughts fill our minds, but we do not speak about them for fear that they may become real if uttered. Our eyes stay glued to the door.

Finally, in the late afternoon, we hear the

familiar footsteps coming briskly down the hall. The door opens and there stand our two brothers. They are smiling.

The judge had compassion. He was touched by the courage and devotion of a young child like Moishele. He was impressed by Motele's moral strength, for he did not reveal the names of the others and thereby saved their lives. The punishment for stealing was deportation to slave labor camps.

Motele's sentence: cleaning the outdoor toilets for two weeks.

15

Spring arrives. The air is fresh and warm. Pesach is here. How different Pesach is now. There is no painting the apartment, no scrubbing the floors, no hustle and bustle.

Mama is gone. It is hard to believe that there was a time when this home was alive, buzzing with holiday joy, with people, with love. Was it only four years ago, just before Pesach, that Mrs. Gruber was poking her head through the front door, reminding Mama to make a peasant shirt for her grandson, Harry, to get matzos for Pesach?

How far away it all seems now. Where is Mama? Is she alive? Can she survive without her children? She always lived for us.

Mrs. Gruber's life has changed so drastically. But is it for the better? Her son has been drafted into the German army, her grandson sent to the German front. Will Harry become one of the war victims? One more number killed for "the Fatherland." I think about him a lot; about his mother, Olga; about his grand-mother. We are all losers. Still, nature is alive; life goes on. . . .

In the midst of Pesach, the holiday of freedom, the holiday of joy—in the midst of nature renewing life, Laibele's life ends.

I refuse to let him go, shaking his body, screaming, calling to him, "Open your eyes, Laibele! Keep fighting! Do not give up!"

He opens his eyes, closes them, and opens them again. His eyes sadly apologize for not being able to struggle anymore. I hold him in my arms, keep on talking to him. There is so much we still have to say. "Laibele, please do not leave us. Please, darling, please."

The neighbors come running. They pull me away from his bed. "Please, don't let him die! Don't let him die!" I wail.

Mrs. Avner puts her arms around me, holds me close, speaking softly but sternly: "Riva, you are sinning. You are not letting him die in peace. You are calling him back, again and again. This is a great sin you are committing. Let him go, darling. Maybe he will be better off than we are."

the cage

I hear a deep sigh coming from Laibele's chest, and he is silent. He is gone. He closes his eyes forever.

Again Motele, Moishele, and I cuddle together to find the courage to go on, to comfort one another.

Now we are only three.

The wagon that picks up the dead comes the next day. They take Laibele's young body and leave. Our home is silent and empty. The sun does not stop shining.

16

He is standing in the doorway when I first see him, tall, skinny, with sandy blond hair covering his forehead. His blue eyes gaze straight at me, studying my eyes, searching for a special way to start our acquaintance. A forlorn kind of grin plays around his mouth as he says in a quiet voice, "I am Yulek Schwartz. I was sent here by the Skif. What can I do to help?"

I look at him in surprise. I have never met him before. I have grown up in the socialist movement, and I know most members of Skif, the children's socialist movement. We meet often, study, plan for the future, help to hide people about to be deported. But I have never met Yulek.

He must have read my mind. "I am new to the group. I was told about you, Motele, and Moishele." He halts for a moment, then says, "I know about your mother and Laibele." He presses my hand with gentle warmth.

He comes every evening, sometimes bringing along his sister, Faygele. She is fourteen, Yulek seventeen.

"I know how you feel, Riva, but you are not the only one, if it helps any," he says in his calm, tranquil voice. "My father was taken from us that bloody Thursday in April 1940."

"My God!" I gasped. "The horror caravan. I was there. He could have been one of those men who called out last regards, names, addresses, messages to their families. Maybe I ran right next to him. Maybe I looked at him without seeing. He could have been just another mask of horror among the other painstricken faces."

Yulek puts his hand on mine and strokes my fingers gently. "My mother"—he swallows hard—"lost her mind. She was placed in the mental hospital. Faygele and I would go to see her often, but she did not know us. She locked herself in a world of her own. We were not part of her world. Maybe she was at peace. The Nazis deported her from the ghetto when the first transports of the sick were taken. You know, the hospital was the first to go. So, you see, I am father and mother to Faygele—just as you are to Motele and Moishele."

His very presence makes us all feel calmer, more composed. His voice, soft, kind, full of quiet determination, inspires us. What secret power is giving him that hunger for life, that will to survive that he passes on to all around him?

Yulek always has a book hidden under his shirt. He reads poetry to me for hours, begs me to keep on writing my journal, my letters to my family. "You see, Riva, someday it will all end, and those letters will be very important. We may forget what has happened today, but your letters will remember."

"But, Yulek," I argue, "those letters will never be mailed. They may die here together with us. Why write them?"

Anger rises in his soft, blue eyes. "Don't you ever speak to me that way! Don't ever speak of dying! You are giving up? Don't you ever, ever give up. There is a tomorrow for us! We will live to tell our story to the whole world. We must teach mankind what evil, hatred, and prejudice can do. We must make a better world by not letting them forget what has happened here. So, you keep on writing, and never stop being yourself." He lowers his voice and touches my hand softly. "I am sorry for shouting. You made me so angry, talking the way you did."

I am sorry that I made him angry. I feel guilty for giving up.

I look around me. This was the home of my grandparents. This was the home of my mother, my aunts, my uncles. This was the home of my sisters, my brothers. They all left traces of their lives here, between these walls. How can I think that they will never return? How can I think that we will all just vanish from here? I must continue. They have a right to know what happened while they were gone. They left me in charge. They are counting on me. I must never again give up. Yulek is right.

I put my hand on top of his and smile.

17

An order comes from the ghetto government. We must vacate our home within a few weeks. The building we live in is going to be torn down and used for firewood. We have expected this to happen. Still, it shakes us up.

The ghetto suffers a shortage of heating supplies. The cold in the homes brings more sickness and more death. The ghetto population is getting smaller and smaller. To help the people to survive, the older buildings are being torn down and used for heating.

I look around me. This place has been our home all our lives. My entire family fills the house with memories. I feel Laibele's presence around us. I hear his sweet, gentle voice. *Courage, my dear sister, courage.*

Motele and Moishele speak very little as we pack our belongings. We all know in our hearts that we are attending a funeral. There are no words to ease the pain. We are the last three survivors of our family, parting forever with the traces or our childhood, with memories that still live here.

I stare at the empty house. My feet stay nailed to the floor, refusing to take the last step that will cut us off from here forever.

Yulek takes my arm gently, walks me to the door. "They will always live in your heart and mind. You are taking them all with you," he says.

Our new home, a one-room walk-in, was once a small grocery store. It has a front and back entrance and a very large cellar.

"It may be of great value to us," Motele says while he examines the huge, clay opening in the floor. "It is big and deep. It will make a good hiding place from the Nazis. Just think: This place that was used to store potatoes, vegetables, coal—this dark, cold hole—will now be used to hide people for as long as possible."

I listen to the sound of Motele's voice and try to picture this place filled with sacks of flour, sugar, rice, beans. This cellar filled with vegetables. Shelves of bread and rolls. Buckets of milk, butter, eggs. And people: mothers with children by their sides, buying food for their families, busy with their daily chores.

Where are they all now? Where are the mothers? Where are the small children? Where are the people whose voices filled this room?

"Riva!" Moishele startles me. "Are you wandering in the past again? What were you thinking of?" He looks at me with so much warmth, this sweet, young child who never had any childhood.

He was only eight years old when the Nazis marched into Lodz. They crushed his world. He is twelve now, an orphan with a heart full of sorrow but also love and tenderness. A gentle soul, full of hope.

"Riva, this is our home now. Life must go on." He swallows hard. "Let's get organized. Let's keep going."

I put my arms around him and hold him close. I kiss his light brown hair.

"I am so lucky to have you two, my wise and darling brothers. I still have you two to hold onto. I love you both so much."

Moishele touches my hand, slightly embarrassed by my show of emotion.

"We love you, too, Riva, but let's not get mushy. We have work to do." But his voice betrays the fullness of his heart.

the cage

Motele puts his arms around Moishele. "Hey, look at those shoulders," he says with a twinkle in his eyes. "Boy, you are growing so big. Much too big for all that mushy stuff. But you are just big enough to move furniture around. So let's get going. Let's start with the beds. How about putting them against the wall over here?" He points to the wall on our right and stops, his eyes fixed on the corner of the left wall as if writing invisible to our eyes but clear and calling to him were written there.

"The library! The secret library!" he cries out with excitement. "This corner will be perfect for it! Look closely. It is right near the back door. Easy for people to come and go without the neighbors noticing. We'll put curtains over the shelves, and it will look like a closet. Riva! Moishele! Let's do it! Let's bring the library over to our house!"

Moishele and I look at his radiant eyes, burning with an inner flame. We, too, feel his excitement. We, too, are caught up in his vision. The library!

It took so long for the members of the adult socialist movement, the Bund, to get the library together. Young and old, risking their lives, slowly collected, slowly salvaged hidden books that were not burned by the Nazis, forming the secret library.

Books are not allowed in the ghetto. Still, they are here! We read. We study. We learn and we draw strength from the books.

The library is hidden at the home of the Rosenfarb family now. But its popularity, the traffic it brings to the Rosenfarbs', is putting those kind, dedicated people in constant danger. The time has come to move the library to a different place.

Learning takes the place of food now. The books give us hope, strengthen our will to live, to plan for a better, brighter tomorrow. The knowledge they bring to our hungry minds gives new energy to our weak bodies.

We cannot give up the library. But what price do we have to pay to house it? We must put our lives in danger. Motele's, Moishele's, my own.

I look at Moishele. I look at Motele. Their faces show no fear. Only determination. They are waiting for a sign of my approval.

"Well, someone has to do it, so why not us? Why not here?"

The boys from the woodworking shops steal wood for the shelves piece by piece, risking their lives with each little board they smuggle out of the shops. I make curtains from fabric that Mama never had a chance to use up. I wonder, What would Mama say if she knew what we were doing? I think she would approve.

Slowly but surely, a few books at a time, we move three hundred books to their new home at 18 Berka-Joselewicha Street.

18

Our home becomes a very active meeting place. While exchanging books, we also exchange bits of news. Who has been placed on the latest list for deportation? How can we save our friends? What can each of us do to help?

If we can only keep off the list. Hold on. Keep on going. The day will come. The day of freedom, of a new life. The burning issue: how to keep on hiding if one's name is on the list.

Often our home holds sudden guests. Three people in each bed. Others on the floor, huddled together, listening for strange knocks at our door. If we are found hiding someone, we will be taken. But there is always the hope that we will not be caught. We must take the chance. Someday we, too, may be in the same position. We would want others to help us.

Our cellar stands ready and waiting at all times. Blankets and pillows are spread out on the clay floor. Often our friends hide in the cellar for hours while we wait for the house to be searched by the Jewish police. With pounding hearts we listen for their heavy footsteps. We hold our breath each time someone passes our door. Will they stop at our door or go on? Are they looking for someone? Are they looking for us? Is this our last night here?

At the tailor shop on Brzezinska 50, where I have come back to work, the cutting department is in an uproar. My coworkers look very upset. I hear angry whispers and feel icy glances following me. What is happening? My eyes dart from one face to another, searching for an answer. They are all avoiding me. Why? Why? Why?

We have always had such a close and warm relationship. We are a small group holding together like a family. I am the youngest and looked after like a kid sister by all of the others.

I was put into this specialty group, the cutting room, by the shop manager, David Berkenwald. He knew my parents from their union activities before the war. They had worked together in the tailor trade. Each time he passed me in the huge hall where I worked before, bent over the sewing machine, he stopped. He touched my hair gently and said, "Rifkele, that machine is bigger than you are. You look so lost here. Those military coats are much too heavy for you. You are too small and much too young for this department. I must find something else for you, something a little easier. You will collapse by this machine if I do not move you soon. Motele told me about your gall bladder and about your weak legs. I have to get you out."

One day I *did* faint. I had a severe gall bladder attack. There was not much I could do but suffer in silence and hope that it would pass soon. Maybe it would be the last attack.

They carried me to the first aid station, revived me, and a while later sent me back to the sewing machine, still doubled up in pain, tears flowing silently from my eyes.

The next day Mr. Berkenwald moved me to the cutting room. "You will help lay out the fabric for the cutters. This work is not as hard as the other. The people in the cutting department are very nice. They will take care of you. I already told them about you. We must help one another to survive."

The people are truly kind. They took so

much interest in me and my younger brothers. They all took personal pride in our strength to hold on, in our determination to study, to help one another, to help others. They admired our courage to hide a library in our home. Sometimes they asked to borrow books, and on days when the mood was a little lighter, I would tell of books I had read. They liked the stories I shared with them. Life in the shop was so much easier, so much nicer with those people. Until today.

Now there seems to be a cold, invisible wall standing between us. A chill fills the room. I feel their resentment. But why? What did I do?

I cannot stand it any longer. I turn to a tall, pale woman in her thirties with black hair and dark, sad eyes. She lost her two children. They were taken away by the Nazis one day. Her sorrow is written all over her face. Sometimes she puts her arms around me, hugs me close, cuddles me like a child in her arms. "You are a child without a mother," she says. "I am a mother without children."

"Miriam," I ask, "what is happening here? Did I do something wrong? Please tell me."

She takes my hands in hers. They are ice

cold. I feel her trembling fingers touching me. "I thought you knew," she says slowly, with a choked-up voice.

"Knew what?" My heart is pounding violently. "What am I supposed to know? Did something happen to Motele? Moishele?"

She caresses my hair. "Nothing happened to them. Nothing happened to them. It has to do with you. You were on the list of teenagers to be deported." She stops. "Each shop had to give a list. But Berkenwald removed your name from the list. He put someone else in your place."

I stare at her without seeing. My head spins. My thoughts race one after the other. Should I laugh? I am not being deported. Should I cry? Someone else is going in my place. Should I feel happy? Should I feel guilty? I bury my head in my hands and cry.

"Riva. Stop crying." Mr. Berkenwald is standing behind me. He puts his hands on my shoulders. His voice is tense, filled with emotion. "Look at me. You have to know why I made such an awesome decision. You must try to understand."

I look at his face, pale, drawn, distressed.

He has become so much older in one day. I see the pain and sorrow in his eyes.

"Riva, I had to do it. I had to play God. I had to choose. The list called for teenagers, true, but you are only a teenager in years. In reality you are a mother of two younger children. You are the legal guardian of your brothers. I did not save one life—I saved three. Your brothers would go with you if you were deported. They would volunteer. They are so young. What chance would they have in a labor camp? You are their mother; you must protect them! You must think of them! I did. . . ."

Tears flow down his face. I bury my face in his chest and cry hysterically. He caresses my hair gently.

19

"Mr. Berkenwald was right." I hear Motele's comforting voice. "He saved three lives. He was right. We would never let you go alone, and he knows it. We must hold on to one another. We must hold on to life. So be grateful for the chance he gave us to stay together. Life is cruel in the ghetto . . . but it must go on. It must go on."

I repeat slowly, "Life is cruel. . . . Life is so cruel. . . . We cry for the ones we lose and continue to live. We eat, sleep, hope, dream, laught, love, and hate. We do not turn to stone and stop feeling. We suffer pain and sorrow and go on living. But there must be a limit. How much can we endure and still say, life must go on."

"We all wish we had an answer." Moishele's soft gentle voice is soothing, calming. "I wish we had an answer, but life does go on. We lost Mama, and we felt that we would never be able to live without her, but we are still alive. We lost

Laibele. . . . We are still alive. You see, Riva, life does go on. It must."

And life does go on.

Yulek comes by every evening. We sit quietly on the sofa, read poetry, and dream of a better world.

His eyes take on a special soft glow each time they meet mine. Do I care for him as more than a friend? I wonder. How does he feel about me? I wonder. I wonder about so many, many things. We never speak about our feelings. It is so pleasant, so peaceful just to be together in a world of our own. A world of poetry, beauty, hope. Forgetting death knocking at our door, we still dream, hold hands, and smile.

Life does go on. . . .

The sun is shining. Spring is again covering the cold earth with a blanket of new blossoms. Nature is awakening, sparkling with new life. The gentleness of spring fills the air. Passover is approaching once again.

When I was a child, it was the symbol of freedom, a time to rejoice. But now it brings only the sad reality that we are still slaves—not in a faraway land, Egypt, but in the land of our birth, Poland. Will we, too, have a Moses to lead us to freedom, as our forefathers did? Is there a Moses among us?

Motele looks at me with a mischievous twinkle in his blue eyes. His lips form a timid, nervous grin.

"I know you are in trouble, my dear brother." I smile with my eyes while trying to sound serious. It is hard to be angry with him. "I know you're hiding something from me. Out with it."

"Well—"

Moishele hastily interrupts. "Remember what holiday is coming?" He, too, is flushed with excitement.

"It is Pesach. So?"

Motele takes over. "Remember what we always got for Pesach when Mama was with us?" His voice cracks for a second. He swallows hard and regains his composure. "Remember the new clothes and what Mama always said? 'Pesach would never be Pesach without new clothes.'"

I have a choking feeling in my chest. I see Mama's smiling face. I hear her words ringing in my ears. *Pesach would never be Pesach without new clothes.* I see her bending over the sewing machine, singing happily while sewing dresses, shirts, coats for her children for Pesach.

My eyes fill with tears as I look at my brothers. They, too, remember Mama's words. She is always with us.

"So," Motele says. "So. Moishele and I decided that it is time for you to get something new for Pesach. You need some new clothes badly. We received new clothes from the Child Welfare Department when you legally adopted us, but you lost your rights as a child. Legally you are a mother. But to us you are our sister who needs a new suit. It would break Mama's heart to see your wardrobe. Real shmattas. Remember, you are a young lady now, and boys are looking at you like—well, like a young lady."

Motele grabs my arm and pulls me toward the closet, opening the closet door with his free hand. "Look in the closet, Riva. What is missing?"

"Why would there be anything missing? Who needs our shmattas?" I ask.

"What do you mean, shmattas!" Moishele exclaims. "How about Uncle Baruch's gray tweed coat? You call that a shmatta?"

"Oh, that. Well, that was a beautiful coat once, rich and elegant, with fur inside and on the collar. All that's left is a gray tweed fabric, a reminder of different times, before the Germans confiscated all the furs that belonged to Jews."

Uncle Baruch . . . Uncle Baruch . . . I feel like screaming. Our beloved uncle. Talented. Handsome. Bright. The pride and joy of our family. Mama's younger brother. She raised him and helped him become an educator. Such a happy, warm human being. Where is he now? He left with his wife, Eva, and their baby, Rutka, to escape the Nazis, just as my sisters and brother did. Where is he now? Where are they all now? Mama held onto the coat. *He'll need it when he comes back home*, she said.

She is gone now. He is gone. But the coat is still here.

"So where is the coat? Did you put it away in another closet? Mama always loved that coat." I hear myself sigh deeply.

"If Mama were here now," Moishele says slowly, weighing every word, "she would take that beautiful gray tweed coat and make it over into something for her young, growing daughter. I am sure that she would say, 'Uncle Baruch can have a new coat made when he returns, but Rifkele needs a new suit now.' And she would make from the coat a suit for her Rifkele."

"That is right!" Motele cannot hold back any longer. "That is what Mama would do! But Mama is not here, and we have to take over for her. We took the coat to Karola's uncle, the tailor. He will make you a new suit for Pesach! The labor has already been paid! I am sure Uncle Baruch will also approve when he comes back."

"Hold on, boys. Not so fast. Maybe Mama would have done this. But how can we be sure? What right do we have to make use of a coat that is not ours to use? And what do you mean, the labor is all paid up? How did you pay?"

I look from one to the other, my eyes flashing with anger. Did they do it again? Sell their bread? They sold their bread before to get medicine on the black market. They went for a whole week without bread to get the vitamins I needed. Once they sold their bread to buy one tangerine for me, hoping that it would give me strength. Are they doing it again? Paying with bread so I can have a new suit for Pesach? So I can look well dressed?

"No! You cannot give your bread away

again. It is not that important how I am dressed. I will not let you do this!"

Motele puts his arms around me. "We kind of expected it," he says with a grin. "So we gave him the bread last week. You cannot stop us now—and you cannot change our minds. Anyway, we were planning for a while, so each time we divided our daily rations of bread, we made the portions a little smaller, until we'd saved up half a loaf of bread to pay for the labor. So, you see"—he is beaming with pride—"we outsmarted you. And you did not even notice that the portions of bread got smaller."

Moishele puts his hands on my shoulders. "I am so glad that we trust one another, not like some families, who steal one another's bread to fill their own stomachs. I am so glad we are as we are and we have one another." I see tears glisten in his eyes.

How can I stay angry? I put my arms around the two of them, hug them close to me, and cry.

The beautiful gray tweed coat becomes a beautiful gray tweed suit under the skilled hands of the tailor. He looks with pride at the suit he has made and with warmth at my flushed face as I stand in front of his full-length mirror. "Your mama has raised very special kids, Riva. Very special kids."

20

"I am on the list." I read the dreadful words in Yulek's eyes even before he utters them. "My sister, Faygele, is coming with me," he says in his soft, gentle voice.

"Hide! We'll hide you in our cellar! You must hide!" I grab his hands with sudden force. "You cannot go! You must not go! I won't let you go!"

"There is no use, Riva." His voice is breaking as he speaks. "There is no use. Maybe it is all for the better. Faygele is all skin and bones. She cannot hold on much longer here. I have nothing to help her stay alive with in here. Nothing. Maybe it is true what they tell us, that they are sending us to labor camps, where we'll have a better chance to survive this hell. I have no choice. I have no choice."

I look at his sad eyes. What has happened to the sparkle if hope that has always been there? What has happened to his determination to live? What has happened to his strength to fight for each day?

the cage

I swallow the lump in my throat. "Yulek. You must not give up. We know what life in the ghetto is like, but maybe it is even worse outside the ghetto. Maybe we have a better chance to survive right here. We must not give up hope."

"Riva." He caresses my hair softly with his trembling fingers. "Riva, you, at least, must understand. You are the guardian of your brothers. You are legally and morally responsible for their lives. I am the guardian of my younger sister, not legally but morally.

"I promised my mother to look after my sister. As long as I can, I must do it. I must think of her welfare. She is too weak, too delicate to survive in a cellar. I cannot put her in hiding, where she will die from each strange sound. It takes strong nerves to hide. There is no hope for her here. Our only chance may be reporting for transportation to a labor camp. We are young; they need our labor skills. They say that even the weak can be used in the camps, for the easy work. As long as they need us, we may have a chance."

He utters a deep sigh. "We must hope that we are making the right choice. We must hope that this will all end soon."

He looks at me, and there is a glow in his eyes now. "Riva," he says, "you will not forget me, will you?"

I try to manage a smile, taking his hand in mine. "How can I forget someone who reads poetry to me with so much feeling? I'll wait until you return to read again."

He squeezes my hand. "It's a deal. It's a deal."

"Yulek, what can I do to help?" The lump in my throat is back again.

He thinks for a moment and says, a bit embarrassed, "I don't know what to pack for this journey. I can use some help."

I walk into Yulek's apartment with slow, hesitant steps. I have never been here before. How sad and strange life is. My first visit to Yulek's home is to say good-bye to my dear friend—my more-than-friend.

It is a one-room apartment, crowded with reminders of better days. With pictures of loved ones looking down from the walls. A picture of a smiling woman stands on the dresser. Yulek looks like her, blond, blue-eyed. The same gentle smile. She is dead now. This beautiful lady lost her mind. Hid in a world of her own, away from all this horror, and they killed her for that.

I look at Faygele, sitting on the bed, pale and forlorn. Her blond hair is disheveled. Bewildered and lost, she, too, looks like her mother. But there is no smile on her face. There is only fear there. I wonder if that is what their mother looked like when she took sick. My heart breaks looking at her. A gentle, young child surrounded by madness and death.

"Riva, I am so glad you are here. I am so afraid. I am of no help to Yulek. I am so afraid." She stretches her thin arms toward me. "Hold me, Riva. Hold me."

I hold her tightly. She is so helpless. I understand why Yulek must go. He has no choice. He is her strength.

Embarrassed, Yulek points at the open drawers and the clothes scattered all over the room. "Look at this mess here. I told you, I am no good at packing. I am glad you came."

We pack two suitcases, saying very little. We are lost in a world of unspoken feelings. Is this good-bye forever? Why does it have to be like this? Why? Why? Why?

"We must clean up this house before we leave in the morning." Faygele's voice reaches me from a distant world, from far, far away. "And we must lock the door. We do not want anybody to come in here while we are away. Mama always said that you must leave the house clean when you go away, so you come back to a clean house. We will come back, won't we, Riva? We will come back."

"Yes, Faygele. You will come back. You must come back." I look at Yulek now. "You must come back. You must come back," I whisper.

The packing is done. The house is clean. I must leave now, before curfew. Yulek walks me to the door. We stare at each other and suddenly embrace. For the first time we embrace each other. I feel the violent pounding of my heart and the pounding of his as we stay in each other's arms. Our lips meet for the first time. We hold on tightly to each other. We are safe as long as we are together. If only we could stay like this forever. I feel hot tears gliding down my face. I do not want to cry, but the tears keep coming and coming, leaving their salty taste on our lips.

I pull myself away from his arms and run

down the stairs, crying aloud. I feel like screaming, shouting, Why? Why?

Yulek's warm voice trails after me. "I will be
back, Riva. I will be back!"

21

It has been four months since Yulek and his sister, Faygele, were deported from the ghetto. As with all the others before them, there is no news. The mail to the ghetto has long since been stopped. Nothing comes in or goes out. Only people leave—and they never return.

Deportation orders are speeding up. Daily bulletins are placed all over, in the shops, offices, on the street walls. "Leave the ghetto as volunteers," they urge. "You will get an extra loaf of bread. Families who leave together will remain together."

It is a hard decision to make. Before our hungry eyes they are dangling extra bread. It is bait to lure us out, or are they sincere? Will we stay together as families, as they promise? What are we to do?

Questions, questions, so many questions, but no answers. Some, physically and mentally worn out, wanting to believe the daily bulletins that shout at us from every corner, give in and report to the railroad station, a bundle on their shoulder and hope in their heart, trying to convince themselves it's the only way.

Hans Biebow, the S.S. ghetto commander, makes personal appearances at the large shops to present his point.

It is a bright summer day. Not a cloud in the sky. Biebow is coming to the tailor shop where I work. We are all ordered outside to listen to his speech.

Surrounded by S.S. guards and ghetto officials, Biebow looks relaxed. He smiles and speaks calmly, softly: "I came here today, ladies and gentlemen, because I am your friend. I care what happens to you all. You are very important to us. We need your skilled labor. We need your talents.

"Listen to me, ladies and gentlemen. I personally urge you to report to the railroad station for resettlement to a different place of work. We are doing this to protect you from the Russians. The Russian army is coming close to Lodz. They will not think kindly of you. Remember, you made uniforms for the German army. . . . They will punish you for working for us. But we do not want you to suffer. We need you all. We need your labor. You are good workers, and we are only moving you to a safer place so you can continue to work for us. We want to save you from the Russians because we need you.

"Trust me, ladies and gentlemen." His voice is still soft and gentle, and his face is now covered with a broad smile. "Trust me, please. I promise you, not a hair will be harmed on anyone's head. We will keep you together as families if you leave together as families. You can take whatever you can carry. You will have better working conditions. You will be safe. You will be happy. I promise you. We need you."

He sounds so sincere. So honest. So caring. He leaves, still smiling and waving a friendly good-bye.

We stand silent, bewildered. Then everyone starts speaking all at once, agitated: "Maybe he is telling the truth. They do need our labor. Why would they want to harm us? He sounds so honest, but can we trust him? We cannot trust the Nazis! They are murderers! It is a trick! They want to make the deportation easier on them. It will save them the trouble of searching for the Jews if we come on our own. Do not listen to them, friends! Hide! Resist! Do not go freely!"

"Hide? Where can we hide? Resist? With what can we resist? With what can we fight them? We may make it worse by trying to fight. We have no chance against them. We have no chance. Maybe the Germans are losing the war. Maybe they are becoming more human."

Shouts all around me. Feverish, excited voices coming from all directions. Whom do I listen to? Who is right? Who is wrong?

My face is hot, flaming from the inner turmoil. My head is buzzing. What shall we do? What shall we do?

"Riva!" I hear a familiar voice. Mr. Berkenwald stands near me. "Riva, do not trust the Nazis. Hide. Do not report to the railroad station on your own. Hide. Hide."

"Do not volunteer! Do not volunteer! Hide as long as possible!" The message is quickly passed on.

We stop going to work. We stay together with our families. Whatever happens, we'll be together. The Germans surround us and pull people from their homes into the waiting wagons. Screams and cries fill the warm summer air. And the sun does not stop shining.

Our cellar is a busy place now. We keep

blankets and pillows ready on the clay floor at all times. At the sound of German voices from far away, Motele, Moishele, I, and whoever happens to be at our house at the time jump into our hideout. We curl up in the pitch darkness of the cellar like hunted animals and wait for the hunter to leave in search of other victims.

The tension. The stress. The horror. It is nerve-racking. It is unbearable.

The nights are easier. They do not come at night. We use the peace of the night to check up on our friends. Who has been caught? Who has died? Who has managed to live another day?

Our good friends Karola Mikita and her brother, Berl, live only across the street with their mother. Their father was taken away during the horror caravan in 1940. Our friends Laibish Boruchowich and his sister, Rifkele, live on the next street. They lost their father during a Nazi ghetto raid at the time we lost our mother. They live with their mother, who looks upon me as one of her children. Her youngest child, Chanele, my best friend, died of tuberculosis about the same time as my little brother, Laibele. We are all like a loving family, holding on to one another for strength and support.

the cage

What shall we do? The food rations are running out. How can we survive without food? Should we report to the railroad station? Should we try to hold out a little longer? Maybe there is some hope if we are still here tomorrow. Maybe . . . maybe . . .

We try to stay in touch with our friends from the youth movement. But they have no answers, either.

"Jews, out! Jews, out!" The Nazis are back again. It is only dawn, but they are here already. They never come this early. Shouts, screams, outcries of pain fill the air. Moments of silence are followed by, "Jews, out! Jews, out!"

We sleep half dressed, ready to hide the moment we hear it. "Jews, out! Jews, out!"

Motele, Moishele, and I jump from our beds. In seconds, we are inside the dark cellar. Motele pulls the trapdoor, which is covered with a rug and located under the table. It is not an easy job to conceal our hideout from the Germans or ghetto police when they are searching the house. But we have had lots of practice. Motele pulls the covered trapdoor in moments. Precious moments.

"Jews, out! Jews, out!" They are pounding

at our door. "Jews, out! Jews, out!"

The door is being kicked open. The wood is cracking under their heavy bolts. Footsteps are pounding over our heads now. We hear furniture being broken, closet doors being ripped open. "Cursed Jews!" they shout. "They are not here! Jews, out! Jews, out!"

We hold one another's hands, digging into the flesh. We hardly breathe. I close my eyes and see Mama's face before me. *Courage, children. Courage.*

Finally there is silence all around us. No more footsteps above our heads. Are they gone? Is it only a trick? Are they there, waiting silently for us to betray ourselves?

We do not move. The pounding of our hearts can almost be heard. My head is spinning. Like a broken record, the same thoughts keep going around in my mind: How many times do we have to hide like hunted animals? Will our hunters win their hunt? How much longer? How much longer? Forever? Forever?

"I think they left," Motele whispers in my ear. "Do you think we can get out of this grave?"

"No! No!" I feel panic in my heart. My

hands are shaking. "No! No! Let's not move yet. They may be waiting for us. Let's sit still and wait until we are sure."

"All right." He presses my hand. "We'll sit and wait. All right." Cramped together, our arms around one another, we sit and wait. Not a sound is uttered. Has it been minutes? Hours? Days? A lifetime?

Suddenly we hear footsteps above us. Softly, carefully moving about. The table is being moved. We stop breathing. Is this the end for us? A familiar voice breaks the terrifying stillness: "It is all right. They left. I came to see if you are all right."

A warm, friendly hand reaches into the cellar. It is Laibish. He has come to see if we survived the latest raid. "We are all still here. They did not find any of our friends," he says quickly to answer the unspoken question.

"How much more, Laibish? How much more?" I whisper.

He puts his arms around me. "We must hold out. We must."

22

We live in constant terror of being caught and separated. The Nazis are emptying the ghetto quickly, with brutal force. The food rations are running out. We have no weapons to fight them with.

For five years we have fought for survival and dignity, living like human beings in spite of the savagery around us. I look at the closed curtains that hide the books, the source of our strength. They nourished our minds even while our bodies were withering. They helped us believe in a better tomorrow. What do we do with them? What will happen to the books now?

As if reading my thoughts, Moishele says, "Riva, the books will survive. Knowledge cannot be killed. Look at these books. We have kept them from perishing in the flames for five years. They have kept us from perishing morally. They will survive."

"You are right, my dear brother. Ideas cannot be killed. The books carry the beautiful ideas of freedom, justice, brotherhood. The Nazis may destroy the books, but the wonderful ideas for a better world will survive. We'll let the books stay right here, on hidden shelves in an empty ghetto, to remind the Nazis of the spirit they could not destroy."

"I spoke to the others of our group last night," Motele says, his voice tired and low. He tries to stay in touch with all our friends. He was almost caught several times during the raids, trying to help others stay alive another day. I often wonder where his determination to live comes from. But his voice sounds strange now. Beaten.

"We have no choice. We have no food. The Nazis will find us soon. There are not too many people left in the ghetto. This makes it easier for them to round up the ones who are still holding out, like us. If they find us, we may lose our lives. We have no choice."

His eyes are so full of pain and anger. "We must remember, we tried to resist as long as we could. We resisted every way possible. If we stay here we will die. But we want to live. We must live. The only chance to survive may be to come out of hiding on our own. We will have to hope that we will stay together if we go together to the railroad station."

We look at one another, searching for reassurance. For a glimpse of hope. For strength.

I turn to the window to hide my tears. It is a beautiful, sunny August day.

"When are we leaving?" Moishele asks, trying hard to control his emotions. "We have to pack some things to take with us."

"If we are still here tomorrow morning," Motele says slowly, "Karola, Berl, and their mother, Mrs. Mikita, Laibish, Rifkele, and their mother, Mrs. Boruchowich, will all come here. We will all leave together, as a family. We must hope that we will remain together. We must hope. . . ."

"So, what do we take, Riva?" Moishele pulls me gently away from the window. "We cannot give in to despair. It will not help. Remember: If hope is lost, all is lost."

"If hope is lost, all is lost," I repeat after him.

I look around me, taking in the familiar surroundings of our home. Every detail, every corner. This will all have to live in my memory until we return. I want to take everything with me on our journey, all those precious details. I must carry them in my heart.

In our hands we can carry only our personal belongings. What do we pack? Where are we going? For how long? How do we walk out with only a bundle in our arms?

"Should we take some family pictures?" Moishele asks, looking lovingly at Mama's portrait hanging on the wall. She looks so beautiful, her dark hair parted in the middle, a gentle smile on her lips, her blue eyes so soft and dreamy.

"Well, just a few," I say, looking at Mama's portrait. Maybe we will find her somewhere on our journey, alive and well. Maybe she is waiting for her children with outstretched arms.

If hope is lost, all is lost. I hear Mama's voice.

Motele pulls open drawers filled with my poems, my journal, my letters to our mother, sisters, and brother. He looks at me. "Riva, I think we should take all your work with us. It may be safer with us than left behind in the house."

I glance at the written pages lying neatly in the drawer, waiting to tell the story of our struggle for life, for dignity.

"Motele, we cannot take all my work. We must not. If Mala, Chanele, and Yankele should return home before we do, they will at least have something to welcome them. These writings will bring them regards, loving regards from their sister and their brothers. They will learn what has happened to Mama and to Laibele. They will know that they were always with us in our hearts. And—if—we cannot return, this will be our legacy."

"Riva, remember, if hope is lost, all is lost," Motele and Moishele say in one voice.

"I remember. I remember," I whisper, while packing my journal carefully into my bag of clothes to take on our journey to the unknown.

23

We spend the night talking. Sleep will not come. We wait for a miracle to end this nightmare. But no miracle comes. The sun rises warm and bright. The bloody Nazi raids begin again.

A knock at the door; our hearts skip a beat. "Do not be afraid, children. It is Chanele's mommy. Open up, please." I hear a soft, familiar voice. Chanele's mommy. As if we would not know her as Mrs. Boruchowich. She is always Chanele's mommy, even though her Chanele is gone, dead.

Motele opens the door. Mrs. Boruchowich, her daughter, Rifkele, and her son, Laibish, the remnants of a large family, stand in the doorway with bundles under their arms. Mrs. Boruchowich is only in her forties, but she looks so much older now. She stretches her arms toward me. "My dear little girl, my dear child."

I wonder if she is speaking to me or to her

Chanele. I hold tightly to her and feel my mother's arms around me.

"Riva," Mrs. Boruchowich whispers, "I hope we will always be together. You are all my children. I can not live without my children."

I feel a lump in my throat. I remember Mama. She, too, spoke those words, only a few weeks before the Nazis took her from us. I swallow hard. "We must hope, Mrs. Boruchowich. We must hope."

She touches my hair with trembling hands. "My Chanele always had hope." She speaks as if to herself. "My Chanele always had hope. She waited hopefully for the day when she would be freed, for the day when she would be well. The day never came. . . . She is in a cold, dark grave now, and I am going away, leaving her all alone here. Who will cry at her grave now? Who will sit at her grave and speak to her when I am gone?"

Her tears pour freely over her dried-out cheeks. "And your little Laibele, who will come to his grave? We are leaving these children behind."

"It is only for a while, Mama. It is only for a while." Laibish puts his arms around her. She buries her gray head in his chest, sobbing violently. He kisses her head softly.

Slowly we take our bundles in our hands. Trying to prolong the departure. Again my eyes rest on the bookshelves. *They will survive.* Moishele's words echo in my ears. *They will survive.*

We lock the door and walk slowly outside the building in deadly silence, like a funeral procession. Karola, Berl, and their mother are waiting in the street for us. "We felt it would be easier on all of us to just meet in the street and go," Berl says, as if apologizing for not coming into the house. "Let's go."

From other buildings, small groups of people with bundles on their shoulders or in their arms are slowly moving into the street. We are not the only ones still here. We are not the only ones leaving today.

I see an old friend of the family. He is a tailor. On his shoulder he carries the head of a sewing machine. He approaches our group. I stare, speechless, at the sewing machine on his shoulders. All machines had to be surrendered to the Nazis long ago.

"I held on to the head of the machine. I

kept it hidden." He answers my unspoken question. "I kept it for the day when there is a world again and I have to start a new life. What is a tailor without a sewing machine? But I figure it may help me now to have a machine. Maybe I will get a better job if I bring my own tools."

We all walk together. Shots echo from the distance. A parade of ghosts marches through a city of death. Empty homes bid us their last good-bye.

24

The railroad station is packed with people. Bundles, sacks, cartons, neatly tied packages all around us. A whole city is leaving on a mass pilgrimage. "Where to? Where are we all going? What is the name of the place? Does anyone know?"

"Please stay together," Motele urges us. "Let's not lose one another in this crowd."

"Children, my dear children, hold on to one another," pleads Mrs. Boruchowich. "We must stay together, children. We must."

On the tracks, freight trains are waiting. They are cattle cars.

"Why cattle cars?" someone asks, full of panic. "We will suffocate in there from the heat. It is mid-August. The heat will kill us."

"What did you expect?" I hear another voice. "You thought they would send us first class?"

"To them we are animals," one voice cuts in sarcastically. "Besides, they want to make sure that these animals cannot escape. They need our hands to make them uniforms. They need our skilled labor. . . ."

"Keep still! Keep quiet! Do not push! You will all get into the wagons! We have plenty of trains for you!" call the guards.

I look around me, search for familiar faces. We wave good-bye to people we know. They wave back. Eyes meet, petrified, aghast.

"What choice do we have? What can we do other than go into the cattle cars? We have no way out, no choice."

People all around me, desperately trying to find an answer. Clinging to tiny sparks of hope. Optimistically spreading rumors: "They stopped the deportation. The Russian front is too close. They are sending us back home. They need us. They will not hurt us as long as they need our labor."

But the trains keep filling up with people. Each wagon is locked. One train pulls away, and another pulls up, ready to be loaded. We wait our turn, holding on to one another.

"Next. Hurry up! Get your bundles! Move! Move! Get into the wagons! You there, hurry, you stupid Jews."

They are calling our group. Panic seizes me. This is it. We are going into the cattle cars for a journey to the unknown. The guards are getting very impatient. They are already bored with the game of loading Jews into the wagons. They are angrier and louder now: "Jew, make it faster!"

Laibish is helping his mother up into the wagon. She slips. He pulls her quickly into the wagon before the whip of the angry Nazi can touch her body. "You cursed old Jew," the Nazi guard shouts, swinging his whip in all directions.

We move fast, trying to duck the whip. So many families are being separated. We must try to stay together. We must try. We are at the end of the line. The train is almost full.

Whatever happens, please let us stay together, I pray silently. Just let us be together.

Someone reaches out to help me up into the cattle car. Motele and Moishele are behind me, lifting me up. They jump in after me.

"Are we all here?" I call out to Laibish.

"Yes. Yes. We all made it into the same wagon. There is Karola, Berl, Mrs. Mikita, my mother, and my sister." He points to the corner of the car. "Let's try to make our way toward them."

We squeeze through the crowded wagon. We sit down on the floor, worn out from the horrible ordeal but relieved to be all together again. We can hardly move our arms. We are just like one big mass of tired flesh, hot and steaming. The doors are about to close. I hear someone scream: "I am part of a family. Don't leave me behind!"

"Here, stay with your family!" I hear a sarcastic remark in German, and someone is pushed into the wagon. The doors close. We are all in total darkness. Some cry out hysterically; others pray aloud.

Slowly my eyes penetrate the darkness. From some cracks in the walls rays of light break through, throwing ghastly shadows on our terrified faces.

"Is this what a grave feels like?" someone wonders aloud.

"In a grave you have more room than this," a sobbing voice answers.

"We must have hope. We must not give up hope." I hear a voice from the other end of the wagon. "Remember all the Hamans who tried to destroy our people. We survived. God will not abandon us now. He will not forsake us. Hope, people, hope!"

"Oh, he's lost his mind completely," someone responds.

I cannot see any faces. They are all covered in darkness. I see only shadows around me. But the voices are clear, painfully clear.

"So, where is God? Why does he not answer us? Have we not suffered enough? What is he waiting for?"

"You are sinning with that kind of talk. We must pray, pray."

"Maybe I have sinned, but what about my little children? What sins can little children commit? They were only babies. Why did they take them from us? Why did God allow this to happen?"

Bitter voices, angry, heartbroken, wailing.

We sit huddled together, listening to the voices around us. Mrs. Boruchowich puts her head on her daughter's lap, mumbling something to herself. Rifkele caresses her mother's head, whispering, "It's all right, Mama."

"Riva." Motele turns toward me, taking my hands in his. His voice sounds so strange. "Riva, they may separate us. They may separate the men from the women. Remember, if this

143

happens, stay with Karola and Rifkele. You must look out for one another. You must be strong. We must live. We must survive. I'll take care of Moishele, I promise. Laibish, Berl, and I are the older boys. We'll keep Moishele between us so he'll look older than thirteen. We'll take care of Moishele. I promise you."

I pull them both close to me. We cry silently together.

Mrs. Boruchowich raises her head from her daughter's lap. "I will watch over my children. I will watch over my children," she says with sudden determination. "Don't worry, my children. Don't worry."

Moishele turns suddenly toward Rifkele. He puts his hand on Rifkele's shoulder. "Rifkele, please take care of my sister," he says. "You are the oldest of the girls here. You are their big sister. Riva is not very strong. She always had us to watch over her. We are leaving her in your hands. Please, look after her."

"I will, Moishele. I will," she whispers softly.

Days turn to nights and nights into days again. The cracks in the walls let in some rays of sunlight to tell us it is a new day. The rays of moonlight coming through the cracks let us know it is night again. We doze, resting our heads on one another's shoulders, awaken startled by nightmares to find that the nightmares are real.

The stench of human secretion mixed with the sweltering heat makes it hard to breathe. The buckets used as toilets are overflowing. People faint from the smell, from the heat, from exhaustion. The trains stop several times, but no doors are opened.

"How much longer? How much more can we endure?"

"Hold on. Do not give up. We will survive." Voices of strangers, trying to comfort one another. Searching for the courage to stay alive.

It has been three long, horrible days and three terrifying nights. "Where are we going? Where are we going?"

The train stops. The doors finally open. The sudden sunlight is blinding, but our ears are filled with music. Music all around us.

"Where are we? What is this place?"

"Welcome to Auschwitz, Jews." A German voice comes through a loudspeaker. "Welcome to Auschwitz, Jews."

The living crawl out. The dead are pulled out.

PART TWO

25

"Men to the right! Women to the left! Quickly! Quickly!" The guards push us with their rifles. "Faster! Move! Faster! Move! Left! Right! Left! Right!"

Everything is happening so fast, like in a horrible dream. The people behind me are pushing me forward toward the women's group, but where is Moishele? Where is Motele? They were near me only a moment ago.

"Moishele! Motele!" I cry out hysterically. "Where are you? Don't leave me. Let's stay together. Don't leave me alone. Motele! Moishele! Motele! Moishele!"

They are lost in the crowd of dazed people. I cannot see them anymore. I keep on calling, "Where are you, my brothers? Where are you, my children? Don't leave me alone. Motele! Moishele!"

I hear names being called out all around me. Children calling their mothers. Mothers calling their children. Husbands calling to wives their last good-byes. And above it all the German commands: "Left! Right! Left! Right!"

A man in a Nazi uniform is pointing with a white baton toward Mrs. Boruchowich. She is pulled out from our group and to the left of us, where a group of older women and mothers with small children are gathered. Her daughter follows her and is kicked back by a Nazi guard toward our group. I grab Rifkele before she can fall and get trampled by the moving crowd. I hear Mrs. Boruchowich's cries as she, too, disappears from my sight.

"Faster! Faster! Left! Right! Faster! Faster!" I am being carried forward.

"I think I saw my brother, Berl, with Motele and Moishele. They marched by with a group of men." I hear Karola's voice behind me. "They will try to stay together. We must also try to stay together."

Karola is holding her mother's arm. Then we hear "Left!"—and her mother is pulled away from her. "Hold on, my child. Don't lose your courage. Hold on, my child!" And she, too, is gone.

From all sides I hear people calling: "You must not lose hope! You must not lose hope!"

the cage

"You must live!" a woman calls to her daughter as she is pulled toward the group on the left.

My eyes are blurred from burning tears. My head is spinning. And through it all come the voices of strangers calling, commanding: "You must live! You must hope!"

I hope that it is all a horrible nightmare. I'll wake up soon. The nightmare will be gone. My brothers will stand beside me. We will be in a free world.

But the nightmare continues. We are pushed forward toward the unknown by whips whistling in the air, their sharp blows landing on the heads and shoulders of the women. Outcries of pain echo all around us.

Karola, Rifkele, and I try desperately to hold on to one another. We are pushed into a long barrack and ordered to undress: "Drop all your clothes and put them in neat piles! Leave all your belongings! Remove your eyeglasses and leave them here! Move forward! Move!"

I move like a zombie. I remove my eyeglasses, which I have worn for the last few years, and feel as if I am suddenly blind, left all alone in the darkness. I am pushed forward, forward.

My head is shaven by a woman in striped prison clothes. "This is to keep the lice out of your hair," she says sarcastically, while cutting into my long, brown hair with her shaver. I stare at her without really seeing her.

There are mountains of hair all around us: blond, brown, black. Piles of shoes, clothing, eyeglasses surround us, each pile growing bigger and bigger with each passing row of new arrivals.

"Quickly! Quickly! Forward to the showers! Move!" We are pushed into a large room filled with showers. Suddenly the water from the shower head comes at me in full force. The cold spray helps to bring me out of the stupor I have been in. I look at my friends, at their shaven heads, at their horror-filled eyes.

I grab Karol's hand. "Karola, is that you?" I whisper. We stare at each other for a long moment.

"Is that you, Riva? Is that you?" She gasps, transfixed by the sight of my shaven head.

"Out! Out! Quickly! Out!" We are herded outside. The sound of the whips makes us move as fast as we can. We are pushed into the bright sunlight of the warm August air stark naked. With my arms I try to cover my nakedness. My cheeks are hot from embarrassment. I feel so degraded.

Someone is handing out one piece of clothing to each girl to cover our naked bodies. I receive a petticoat big enough to wrap myself in. I look at Rifkele next to me. She is tall, and the blouse she received hardly reaches to the end of her buttocks. I pull off my petticoat and hand it to Rifkele. "I am small, Rifkele. Take this. Your blouse will be big enough to cover me to the knees."

She takes off her blouse and puts it on me lovingly. With tears in her eyes she says, "We are not animals yet. We still have our pride."

"March into the barrack! Quickly!"

We walk hurriedly into the huge barrack. It is filled with triple-decker bunks. On most decks lie five shriveled bodies with hungry, horror-stricken eyes. Some bunks are not filled yet.

"Where are you from?" parched lips whisper. "Are there still Jews alive outside this hell? Did you see the smoke? Did you see the chimneys? Do you feel the Angel of Death touching you? Can you smell the burning flesh?"

Those eyes, those voices are so unreal, so

ghastly. This has to be a nightmare.

"Leave them alone." The voices go on and on. "Leave them alone. They will know soon enough about the smoke, about the smell. . . ."

Why doesn't the nightmare end? It cannot be true. I will not listen to them. I will not look at them. I cover my ears, but the voices are within me now. I am part of them now.

Rifkele grabs hold of a small, skinny woman in her late twenties wearing a dress that is much too big. She looks familiar to her. They stare at each other in disbelief. "Tola? Tola?" Rifkele cries out. "Is that you? I am Rifkele, Rifkele Boruchowich. My God, what did they do to you?"

Tola's eyes fill with tears. "Rifkele? Rifkele? The beautiful, elegant Rifkele without hair, wrapped in rags. This cannot be you."

They fall into each other's arms, sobbing: "What did they make of us? What did they do to us? Dear God, help us remain human. Help us."

"I lost my children, Rifkele," Tola says suddenly through her tears. "They took them from me. I lost them." She buries her head in Rifkele's chest, howling like a wounded animal.

the cage

Rifkele hugs her close. "I'll stay with you, Tola. We'll stay with you, Riva, Karola, and I."

She is the only one in her bunk. We slide into her bunk and hold one another close.

26

"Out! Everyone, out! Head count! Out! Out!" Within seconds we are lined up outside the barrack. A strange mass of weird-looking creatures, wrapped in rags, barefooted, with shaven heads and eyes bulging from hunger, horror, bewilderment.

"Where are we? What is happening here? What is a head count?"

After hours of standing in the hot sun, weak, half dead, feet buckling under me, I hear a loud, cold voice bellow through a bullhorn, "You are in Auschwitz now."

"Where is Auschwitz? What is Auschwitz?" I hear whispers.

"You are lucky!" the thundering voice shouts. "You are still alive. If you listen to orders, you'll stay alive. If you cannot work, if you are sick, if you do not follow orders, you'll end up in smoke. Do not move without permission! You go to the toilet barrack only when ordered! Listen for orders!"

the cage

You'll end up in smoke. You'll end up in smoke. Those words spin around and around in my head.

Even without my glasses I can see the dark smoke in the distance, rising to the sky. What is that smoke? What did those words mean?

They count the standing bodies again and again. They count the dead bodies on the ground. The count goes on for hours and hours. It is some sort of cruel game they are playing to see who can last longer. Is this their amusement? Are we their playthings?

Late in the day a kettle of hot soup is brought into the field. The famished women all push forward toward the nourishment. "Move back! Wait for orders! Wait for orders!" comes a voice from a bullhorn again.

The women in the front rows are pushed by the hungry crowd behind them. They try to hold them back by leaning backward, but to no avail.

Suddenly the voice on the bullhorn laughs sarcastically. "Give them the soup! Give them the soup!" And the kettle of hot, steaming soup is poured on the women in the front rows.

Piercing screams fill the air.

"Ha, ha, ha! Was the food tasty? Next time wait for orders. Ha, ha, ha! Next time don't be in such a hurry to eat."

Hours later another wagon with a kettle on it appears. No one moves. Fear makes my empty stomach twist. What are they planning now? Another funny game? But this time they hand out some horrible-tasting soup. We gulp it down hurriedly from metal cans.

We are divided into groups and marched to the toilets. I try to stay close to my friends.

"Make it fast! You have five minutes, ready or not! Five minutes and out!"

The toilet consists of a huge barrack filled with holes in the ground, over which the rag-clad women stand with their legs apart, answering nature's call. I stare at them in shock.

I am not going to the bathroom with all those people around. I grab Tola's hand and whisper frantically, "I cannot go! I cannot!"

"My child, you cannot afford to be bashful here." Her voice is sharp and stern now. She takes me by the hand as she would her small child. "Go. Go the nearest hole. Go fast. Do it fast. They do not care. Forget about your pride. Hurry. The guards will chase us out soon, finished or not.

They'll chase us out and the others in. So, hurry, please."

There is warmth and gentleness in her voice as she pulls me toward an unoccupied hole. "Now, hurry. And watch out not to slip into the hole."

I feel like an animal. "Quickly! Quickly! Out! Out! Out!" We are chased out, ready or not. A new group of women, some hardly able to hold out any longer, is waiting to use the holes.

27

We are cramped together on the bunks. The barrack is huge and covered in darkness.

Moaning and groaning erupt suddenly. "Sha. Do not cry," someone says sternly. "They'll come and take you away. Be still, if you want to live. Be still."

Suddenly we hear a sharp, shrill whistle. A command: "Out! Out!"

Quickly we crawl out of the bunks and line up outside. The air is cold. Chills run down my spine. Is it from the cold air or from the unknown peril?

We stay outside for hours. We are waiting. Waiting for what? Waiting for whom?

Slowly night gives way to dawn. We are still waiting. Finally we are ordered back into the barrack, stepping over the bodies of those who did not survive the night's ordeal. We search for familiar faces.

Once in the barrack we cuddle together on the bunk. "Thank heaven, we are still all together," I whisper on seeing my friends. "We are still alive."

"Close your eyes and try to get some rest while you can," someone whispers. "Do not lose time talking. Sleep. Sleep."

I close my eyes and drift off to a different world. I am surrounded by living skeletons, their eyes bulging from their heads and their bony arms reaching out toward me to embrace me. I jump up, horrified. Was I asleep? Or was that real? Cold sweat covers my body.

"Out! Out! Head count!" We are herded out. "Everybody out of the bunks! Quickly! Quickly! The ones left behind will be taken away. Move if you want to live!"

Some do not have to worry anymore: They are dead. Others, half dead, do not care anymore. They lie motionless, waiting for the end to come and free them from this hell.

A young girl near me is pulling the bony arms of a woman on the bunk. "Mama, wake up. You cannot sleep now. We must move outside, or they will take us away. Open your eyes, Mama. Please, open your eyes." She shakes her mother's feeble body. She pulls her from the bunk.

The woman opens her eyes slowly. She is so weak. She looks at her daughter with pleading eyes. "Go, my child. You are young. You must live." She closes her eyes again.

"Mama! Mama! Open your eyes. Do not sleep now, Mama! Please."

"Your mother is gone, child. She is dead. You must live. She told you, you must live. Come."

She is pulled away, held up by some women. She is struggling with them. "Let me stay here with my mother. I want to stay with my mother!" She is carried outside by the arms, still screaming.

We are gathered at a huge field. The sun is hot. We are lined up for our food ration: a slice of bread and some watery coffee. "This will have to hold you until the soup in the evening, if you are still here," says the voice through the bullhorn.

We stand for hours and hours in the hot sun. "Water. Water," beg some. Some women faint and just lie on the ground, waiting to die.

One of the *kapos*—prisoners the Nazis put in charge of other prisoners—turns on a garden hose full blast. The powerful stream of water knocks some off their feet. Hands reach out to touch the water. Mouths open to catch a drop. But the water is shut off as suddenly as it was turned on.

We are sent back to the barrack. The bodies of the dead have been taken away. The empty places are filled with new arrivals.

28

"What are those chimneys we see in the distance? What is that smoke? What is that stench that reaches us? Does anyone know? It cannot be true what they whisper here, that people are being burned in there. . . ."

The same questions plague us all. We lie in our bunks exhausted, too worn out to speak.

I need rest. If I could only get some rest, close my eyes and sleep. But I am afraid to close my eyes. I may not wake up.

I must live, I tell myself. Motele and Moishele need me. I must search for them as soon as we get out of here. I must search for Mama. Maybe they sent her here when they took her away from us. It has been two years. But some people have been here for two years. Maybe Mama, too, has survived. Maybe she is just nearby. I must search for her. I must be strong. I must find them again. I close my eyes and float away with my thoughts.

Sudden thunder startles me. I open my

eyes. Was it a dream? There is silence, then thunder again. It becomes louder and closer. But is it thunder?

The women around me stare at one another in bewilderment.

"They are bombing the camp!" comes a sudden outcry. "We'll die here like rats in this hell. We must save ourselves. We must get outside. Run, everybody! Run!"

Panic takes over. Some women push toward the doors.

"Girls, don't run! Please, don't run! They'll shoot you if you run outside! Stay calm! Control yourselves! Please, calm down!"

A skinny, pale woman, about forty, wrapped in an old bathrobe, runs through the barrack, pleading: "Girls, I beg of you, keep calm. Listen to me. Do not panic. I am Doctor Ginzburg, from Lodz, the lung specialist. Some of you know me well. I met some of your families. I am your friend. I want you to live. I want to live. Listen to me, please. Those are not just bombs you hear outside. They're music to ease our pain. Someone out there is fighting the Nazis. Someone is fighting for our lives. Those sounds you hear are Chopin's music! Those are not bombs: They're freedom calling. Be ready! Rejoice! Sing! Everybody, sing!"

She starts humming a Chopin melody, her voice loud and strong. "Join me, my children! Join me, my sisters!"

Meekly, slowly, as if in a trance, voices join in until the whole barrack is filled with the sound of Chopin.

"Louder, girls! Louder, my children! Raise your voices high," urges Doctor Ginzburg.

The voices gain strength. Then the door rips open. There is a kapo with a club in her hand. She stares at the singing women and turns in rage toward Doctor Ginzburg. "Do you want us all to die? Silence! Silence, you crazy woman." She hits Doctor Ginzburg with her club, knocking her to the floor. She leaves, still cursing.

Doctor Ginzburg is helped up. "I feel sorry for the kapo," she says. "She is one of us. May God forgive her. We must live. We must."

29

"Out! Out! Quickly! Line up! Move!" Rifles are pointed at us. Clubs fall on people's heads and backs. Shoved and kicked, we follow the commands. In and out of the barracks. In and out. Again and again. Day and night. Day and night.

I feel as if I have been running in and out of this barrack for years—years and years. Could it be that it has been only seven days?

I search for familiar faces, for a familiar gesture. If only I had my glasses. Maybe I would recognize someone. I look closely into people's faces. "How long have you been here? Have you ever heard the name Nacha Minska? Does the name sound familiar? She is my mother. Have you seen her?" Several times I run after a woman—so sure it is Mama—but each time it is only a stranger who, like me, is searching.

If they would let us move around freely, maybe I could learn something from the other women. But each barrack is a prison within a prison. And there are so many prisons here.

"Child, if your mother came here in '42, she is either dead or—if she was lucky—in another camp. Stop searching. Stop running after strangers. Save your strength. Stop looking into people's faces with your blind eyes. You will not find her here."

I turn angrily to the woman who so cruelly is trying to deprive me of my dream, of any shred of hope of finding Mama. She is about twenty years old, with the eyes of an old, worn-out woman who has seen it all. She touches my shoulder with her bony fingers. "I do not want to be brutal, child, but these are facts. I have been here for a long time." She stops for a moment, as if trying to remember how long. "Here, it is the labor camp or the chimney. If you stay long enough, it is the chimney. . . ."

"No! No!" I scream hysterically. "My mother is alive! She is alive! I must not stop searching for her!"

She looks strangely at me and walks away, shaking her head sadly.

"Line up! Hurry! Selection!"

I hear Motele's voice: *Riva, walk straight. Do not cry now. You must look strong. You must look healthy. Riva, walk straight, walk fast. You must not cry now.*

I walk forward as if in a trance, not seeing, not feeling. "Left! Right! Right! Left! Left! Left! Right! Move! Move forward!" We move, a procession of skeletons marching before the Nazi officers whose whim will decide who shall live, who shall die. Right: life. Left: death.

I am sent to the right. Karola, Rifkele, Tola are all here. We are pushed into the cattle cars. Again we are on a journey to an unknown destination. Slaves shipped to slave labor camps.

Only one week ago I came to this hell in a cattle car, but I was in the train with my brothers. I still had hope. I still could feel the warm touch of their hands in the darkness of our prison. Now I am all alone. No mother. No brothers. No family. Where are they? Will I ever see them again?

I am all alone. There is no one to live for. What difference does it make if I live or die? There is no one. I am alone. All alone.

Suddenly I feel an arm around my shoulder, hugging me gently. "If hope is lost, all is lost," Rifkele whispers softly. "Riva, your mother always said it. Remember? She never lost hope."

I rest my head in her lap, crying softly.

30

We arrive. The cattle car doors finally open. "Out! Out! Hurry up! Move, you stupid cows!"

They are waiting, their Nazi uniforms neatly pressed. Their rifles are pointed at us. They are waiting. "Line up! Faster! Faster! Dirty Jews!"

We pile out from the dark confinement of the cattle cars into bright sunshine. We line up.

I must stand straight, I say to myself. I must keep my legs from buckling under. I must walk. Keep up with the others. I must hold on. I must reach the end of this journey, and then . . . What, then? What is waiting for us, life or death? It would be easier to give up now. Why wait for death? But I want to live.

The gravel road is long and winding, set amid majestic mountains. Such beauty. I hold my breath. Beauty and horror all around me. The sun shines brightly, playing on the snow-covered mountaintops. How lovely it must be to run freely among such surroundings. How wonderful it is to be free.

the cage

"Forward, march, you dirty Jews!" The crisp mountain air fills with the sound of whistling whips.

I see it from the distance, waiting for us, the new cage. The gates are wide open to let us enter a new hell. A high, electrified fence waits to close us in again. Barracks, long and low, are scattered over a huge field. In the center there is a tall tower. An armed guard waits with his rifle pointed at us.

We look for smoking chimneys, but the sky is blue, clear. No chimneys. No smoke. No ovens. No gas chambers. There are sighs of relief.

We enter the cage, and the gates close behind us. They line us up. The guards take their positions. Deadly silence. We wait.

The gates open again. A woman in a Nazi uniform enters. She is in her thirties, medium height, with neatly combed, light brown hair. Her eyes look coldly and piercingly at the silent group of petrified girls before her. In her right hand she holds a whip, swinging it through the air swiftly as she moves closer. Her left hand holds the handle of a leash. At the end of the leash is a large German shepherd. The dog lunges toward the horrified girls, growling. She pulls the dog closer to her side, calming him, and stops in front of the silent group, slowly inspecting her new prisoners.

"Welcome to Mittelsteine, my honorable ladies." She smiles. "I am your commandant. I expect complete obedience from my prisoners, or you will feel the touch of my whip." Her whip slashes the air with a whistling sound.

"My helper, Fritz, will teach you to obey." She pats the dog gently. "Right, Fritz? We'll teach them to obey."

Slowly she marches back and forth, searching our faces with her icy gaze. I try not to look at her. "I will take one of you to be the camp elder, and some to work in the kitchen. The ones I choose will be responsible for the rest of you. They will be the first to be punished." She swings her whip.

"If you disobey, get sick, steal food, or are too lazy to work, you'll go to Grossrosen. That's where the chimneys are." She pauses for a moment. "This is not Grossrosen, but I could make you wish that you were there. Remember that."

She stops, points at one of the girls. "You, there. The tall one. Come here."

the cage

The girl comes quickly forward, pulling her ragged dress closer around her skinny body. Holding her shaven head high, she stands before the commandant.

"What is your name?"

"My name is Helen, Madam Commandant."

"Look at me when I speak to you!" The whip lands on Helen's shoulder. We all gasp. Helen sways for a second but remains standing.

The commandant raises her whip again, holding it in the air. "Now will you remember to look at me?"

"Yes, Madam Commandant."

"Louder, you cow!" The whip slashes through the air.

"Yes, Madam Commandant."

"How old are you?"

"Nineteen, Madam Commandant!" Helen looks straight at her.

"Do you have a mother?"

"Not anymore, Madam Commandant!"

"Do you have sisters here?"

"No, Madam Commandant!"

"Did you have sisters?"

"Yes, Madam Commandant!"

"Where are they?"

"They took them away in Auschwitz, Madam Commandant!"

"Well, then, you have no one here. No one to steal for. You are the camp elder. You pass my orders to those cows over there. You are in charge. Remember, Helen, it's you or them."

She laughs. The guards join in. "Now, Helen. Your first command: fifty to each barrack. They must all have numbers."

"Girls, wait for your numbers." Helen's voice quivers.

"Louder, Helen!" The handle of the whip lands on Helen's back.

"Girls, wait for your numbers!" Helen's voice is high-pitched. "Please, wait for your numbers."

"Remember your numbers, you stupid idiots! Forget your names! You are numbers now! You are prisoners! Remember your numbers!" The crackling whip echoes her commands.

31

"Prisoner Number 55082. Forget your name! Remember your number!"

How can I forget my name, Riva Minska? How will my family find me? How will we find one another when this is over?

I must remember my number. But I must not forget my name. I must not let them wipe out my name. Riva Minska. Number 55082. I whisper my name and number as I march into the barrack. Riva Minska. Number 55082.

The barrack is lined with wooden bunks all along the walls. The bunks are three rows high, little wooden holes with sacks of straw, waiting for us. There are fifty of them.

"Into the bunks, quickly. Move. One. Two. Three."

My bunk is on the second level. I climb over the bunk below me and crawl into my new home. There is not even room to raise my head. The straw from the bunk above is hanging over me. I feel like I am in a coffin about to be covered. I bury my face in the straw and cry.

A whistle blows, sharp, shrill. "Out! Fast! Line up, you stupid cows!"

I slide out of my cubicle. I must step on the bottom bunk and then jump to the floor. My foot kicks someone below me.

"Watch where you're going.!"

I turn to apologize. It's Tola, my new friend from Auschwitz. We hug each other. It's like finding a long-lost relative.

"Tola, did you see Karola, Rifkele? I cannot see too well without my glasses. Did you see them? Are they in this barrack?"

Tola looks up and down the rows of wooden cubicles, searching for familiar faces.

"Rifkele! Karola!" I call out loud. "Are you here?" I hear others calling the names of friends or relatives.

"Riva! Riva!" Karola's excited voice reaches my ears.

"I am here, Riva! I am coming!" she calls.

Then comes Rifkele's voice. "I am here, Riva!"

"Tola, Karola, Rifkele," I call joyfully. "We are all in the same barrack. Thank heaven!"

"Out! Out! Line up!"

The commandant and the guards are waiting with clubs in their hands. I hear cries of pain as some of the girls are hit while lining up.

The camp elder hands out clean clothing: a skirt, blouse, slip, and shoes. The shoes are made of canvas and wood. We get metal cups, spoons, and canteens, like in the army. We *are* an army—an army of slaves.

Eager to change into clean clothes, we run into the barrack. It feels so good to have something other than the rag I have been covered with for over a week. We pour ice cold water over our bodies to freshen up. It is so long since I washed up that even ice water feels good.

A whistle. "Out! Line up!"

It has been only a few minutes. Some of us did not get to the ice water. We run out—some of us dripping wet, some half-naked, some with shoes in hand.

Numbers are called. My heart is beating fast. My number. Do I remember it? Is it 55082? Yes, it is.

I listen for my number. I hope I do not miss the call. Some of the girls are hit with clubs for not answering when their number is called. "You must remember your numbers, you stupid cows! Remember your numbers!"

The girls whose numbers have been called are lined up and marched away. "Where are they going? What are they going to do with them?" we whisper to one another.

One girl steps forward. "My sister is in that group, Madam Commandant. Please let me go with her."

The commandant raises her club and strikes the girl. "Be silent, you cursed Jew. All of you, back to the barracks!"

The night is long. We listen for sounds from outside. Will the girls come back?

The room is dark. The searchlights from outside throw ghastly shadows as they pass the small window of the barrack. The empty bunks become visible for a few moments, staring at us like the eyes of death.

A whistle. We jump. "Out! Out! Line up!" It's still night. The air is cold. The light skirts and blouses do not keep away the cold mountain air. The guards, dressed in their warm coats, march briskly back and forth, swinging their clubs all the time.

We stand in silence, waiting. After a long, long wait, the gates open. We hear the sound of marching feet. The sound of wooden shoes pounding on the road. The sound comes closer and closer. We see the shadows of an approaching group. Surrounded by guards with their rifles held high, the group enters the camp.

"Are those our girls?" some whisper.

"Yes. Yes. I saw my sister pass by."

They march by us.

"Where were you, girls? What did you do? Is everyone back?" we ask.

"Silence! Silence, you stupid cows."

A shot rings through the air. "Forward, march!"

We are marched toward the open gate while the returning group is lined up outside the barracks.

32

We march. Darkness covers the long, winding road. The headlights of the guards' bicycles throw yellowish shadows on the little white houses scattered along the mountainside. A sleepy, peaceful village, surrounded by tall, majestic mountains.

Our wooden shoes pound against the pebbles on the narrow road. Hidden by the night, we move quickly, without speaking. The beauty of the surroundings, the peace of the sleeping inhabitants must not be disturbed. Even the guards' commands are subdued: "March! March! Faster!"

The walk is long. The wooden shoes feel strange and uncomfortable. The harsh canvas rubs my skin. I feel blisters on my feet. I wish I could walk without the shoes, but the road is full of sharp pebbles. I see others limping.

One girl tries to get the shoes off her sore feet, and a guard's club nearly hits her head. "Don't be so delicate, Jew! You'll learn to walk in those shoes. March! Faster!" The guard rides away on her bicycle.

The blisters on my feet burn like fire. I bite my lips and march.

From the distance a row of low buildings become visible in the early morning light. We march toward the buildings.

I strain my eyes to see. No chimneys.

"Halt! Line up! Five rows! Fast!"

The lines move quickly forward. We march past rows of neatly parked bicycles, gleaming in the morning sun.

We are inside. The building is clean and brightly lit. Rows and rows of machinery and work tables with different metal objects fill the huge room.

"It looks like some sort of factory," I hear someone whisper. Some of the girls are standing by machines. Instructors show them how to use the machines. I hear the shrill sounds of electrical drills. Small metal parts are put under the drills.

How can I work an electric machine? I cannot see well without glasses. Will they send me to Grossrosen?

"Come forward, please." An instructor points to me.

I move toward him.

"This is a drill," he says, "an electric drill. You put the metal part under the drill, check to make sure it is in place, press the switch. The drill does the rest. It must fit perfectly." He looks at me for a second. "Be very careful with this machine. Now try it."

I move closer to the work table. I stretch myself to reach the machine. I can hardly make it. He watches me, grinning. "How old are you, girl?"

"Eighteen." My voice trembles.

He studies my face carefully. "Eighteen. Ha. You're so small, so skinny. You look more like fifteen."

"I am eighteen, sir. I really am."

"Well, maybe. But you cannot reach this machine, girl. You cannot work here, girl." He shrugs his shoulders. "Sorry."

The guard quickly orders me to join a group of girls standing in the corner—rejects, like me. For a short moment I feel relief. They don't know about my eyes.

"March! March!" The guard points to a door at the end of a hall. "March!"

The door opens. Before us lies a dark tunnel. Gas lights hang from the clay walls, throwing yellowish shadows. We step into the damp and muddy tunnel. Pails and shovels stand against the wall.

"Take the pails and shovels and move forward." A man's voice, speaking broken German, reaches us from deep inside the tunnel. I cannot see him. I can hardly see the girls near me.

We move slowly forward. The clay sticks to the wooden shoes. It's cold, wet, and dark all around us.

"Halt! Stay where you are." We stop and wait. "Girls, I am a Frenchman. A slave laborer. We are building here an underground shelter for the Germans to hide from bombs." There is deep resentment in his voice. "My comrades and I do the digging. You will fill the buckets with the clay and pass them on from one to another. The last one in this chain will take them outside." He stops. "Be brave, mademoiselles."

He starts to hum the "Marseillaise," the national anthem of France, the song of resistance. His comrades join in. I know the Yiddish words to it, and I hum along.

33

The days in the clay grave are hard and long.

"Faster! Lift those buckets!" The guard pokes her head through the entrance of the tunnel.

A girl raises her hand. "Madam Overseer, may I please go to the bathroom?"

The guard looks at her with a smile and walks away. The girl drops her hand and lowers her head.

I have to go, too. I try to hold out as long as I can. I do not want to have to raise my hand for permission. But I must. "Madam Overseer, may I please go to the bathroom." The words stick in my throat. I repeat them, louder.

The guard ignores me. My face feels hot. I have waited too long. I cross my legs, pressing them tightly together. I feel a warm flow slowly dripping down my crossed legs. I wish I could die. For once I am grateful for the darkness that surrounds me.

"Everyone, out!" shout the guards.

the cage

We march from the darkness of the tunnel into the bright lights of the factory. The lights sting our eyes. "Line up! Line up!"

The girls from the factory line up together with us. A tall girl of about twenty, with big, brown eyes, marches next to me. I look at her shaven head and wonder what she looks like with hair. She must be a pretty girl.

"March! March!" Our wooden shoes click against the pebbles on the road. It's always dark. We come and go in the dark. Always in the dark. I wonder why.

I lean a bit toward the girl next to me. "My name is Riva. I come from Lodz. I am in Barrack Two. What is your name?"

"I am from Lodz, also. My name is Rosa. I am here with a sister."

"You are lucky. I am alone."

"I am also in Barrack Two. On a very top bunk."

"How are they treating you in the factory, Rosa?"

She is a silent for a moment, then whispers. "The foreman is very kind. He put a piece of bread wrapped in a brown bag into my pocket today, when no one saw him. I saved it for my sister. She is on the other shift. Maybe I'll get a chance to pass it on to her."

We march silently, each absorbed in her own thoughts.

"Rosa, what are you going to do with the brown bag?" I am filled with sudden excitement.

"I don't know. Why?"

"Would you give it to me, please?"

"What do you need a brown bag for?" Her eyes meet mine.

I lower my eyes. "I'd like to use it to write my poetry."

"Poetry? Here?"

"Yes. I wrote before, in Lodz. I left most of it in Auschwitz. If I can put my thoughts on paper, it might help. . . ."

"You know something?" Now she is excited, too. "Maybe your poetry will survive to tell our story."

"Maybe. I just would like to put my feelings on paper."

"I'll try to collect the brown bags the Germans carry their lunches in, after they throw them in the wastebasket. Some fold them up neatly and take them home. I'll keep

my eyes open. But"—she stops suddenly—
"what are you going to write with? You have no
pen, no pencil."

"You're right. I didn't think of that."

"Riva, let's not give up. When the guard is
out of sight, I'll ask the foreman. Maybe he'll
help. All we want is a small pencil."

"March! Faster! March!" echoes all around
us.

My feet seem lighter now, my empty stomach forgotten.

34

The gates of the labor camp are wide open. The next shift of girls waits silently in the field. Fritz growls, pulling his leash angrily as the commandant marches back and forth in front of the columns of girls. I see fear in my friends' eyes as we are marched by.

"Did anyone get into trouble?" I whisper.

"Yes. The whip has been in motion all day."

"Line up, quickly. Head count!" Helen, the camp elder, calls through a bullhorn.

"Bring the thieves forward! Faster!" thunders the commandant, cracking her whip furiously over our heads.

Five girls are brought out from the camp elder's room. I know the girls. Two of them are sisters, Faige and Chane. They are in the same barrack as I. Their faces ashen, they move slowly toward the commandant. She raises her whip and lets it fall on Chane's head. "Now tell them." She points at the columns before her. "Tell them what you did today."

They stay frozen with fear. "Now, you stupid cows! Speak!" Her whip strikes Chane's head again.

"We stole potato peels, Madam Commandant." Chane's voice quivers.

"Louder! I cannot hear you!"

"We stole potato peels from the kitchen garbage, Madam Commandant," Chane shouts. "We stole potato peels from the garbage."

The whip falls again, on her shoulders. She cries out.

Faige screams. "Please, Madam Commandant. Please don't hurt my sister! We were hungry. Please forgive us!"

The commandant raises her whip again and stops it in midair.

"So you were hungry. Ha! So you think you can steal. Ha! I should not hurt her? Well, I won't hurt her." She hands the whip to Faige. "Here, you do the punishing!"

Faige drops the whip and falls on her knees. "Please, Madam Commandant. I stole the potato peels, not my sister. Punish me. Please don't punish her. Please, please."

"Get up, you stupid cow! Pick up the whip. Give your sister twenty lashes, or I will!"

Faige picks herself up, staring in horror at Chane. "Chanele, I cannot hurt you."

Chane, tears pouring from her eyes, whispers, "Faigele, please do it. It will be worse if she hits me."

Faige picks the whip up from the ground and lowers in on Chane's back slowly, softly. "Chanele, forgive me."

"Harder, you cow! Harder! Or I will do it for you!" shouts the commandant. "Every count! One! Two!"

Faige raises the whip up and down. Each time it touches Chane's body, a strange sound tears from Faige's throat.

"Three! Four!" The commandant and her guard call out loud. ". . . Ten! Eleven!"

Each time the whip touches her, Chane curls up silently.

Faige raises the whip again and cries out, laughing hysterically, "Mama! Can you see me, Mama? Can you hear me, Mama? I did not let them hurt Chanele. I love my sister. I did not hurt her. See her dance. Hear her laugh. Come, Mama, take my hand. Take Chanele's hand. Let's dance. Let's sing."

She kisses Chanele's tear-stained face softly.

the cage

Whip in hand, she dances around her horrified sister. "Chanele, Mama came to take us home. Mama is here, Chanele. Let's go home." Then she sits down on the ground, singing softly.

We stand frozen in horror. "She's crazy," the commandant says with disgust. "She's lost her mind. Take them away!"

The camp elder gently picks Faige up from the ground. Chane puts her arms around her sister. "My poor sister. You are better off now than I." They walk toward the camp elder's room, holding hands.

"Now!" the commandant shouts angrily. "Let this be a lesson to all of you. If you steal—" Suddenly she turns to the guards with a triumphant smile. "I did not beat her. Her sister did."

She starts walking toward the gates of the camp, then stops and turns around. "Camp elder," she calls calmly. "No food for anyone today!" She walks out of the gates.

"Quickly! To the barracks!" call the guards, their wooden clubs and whips swinging over our heads.

We run fast to avoid the whips and clubs. Shaken, horrified by what we have just witnessed, we each crawl into our cubicles.

35

"I have something for you." I hear a whisper behind me, as we march back from the factory one evening. I turn my head and look straight into Rosa's smiling eyes.

"Rosa. Where have you been?"

"Keep marching, Riva. The guard is looking in our direction."

I have not seen Rosa since that horrible day when poor Faige lost her mind. I have not seen Faige, either. They say she is kept in the tiny sickroom the doctor uses to help those unlucky enough to become sick here. The doctor is a former medical student with compassion for others.

I often wonder what will become of Faige. No one is allowed more than three days in the sickroom. Will they send her to Grossrosen, the death camp?

"Rosa, I have not seen you since . . ." It's hard to speak of that day.

"I know. They put me on the night shift for

a while. This is my first day back on days. And I was lucky today. I saw a small pencil on the foreman's desk, and I thought of you." She stops for a moment. "I stole the pencil," she says quickly.

"Rosa!" I whisper, horrified. "I don't want you to be punished because of me. Why didn't you ask your foreman? You said he was a kind man."

"Oh, that one took sick, and the new foreman . . .Well, let's say I could get into more trouble by asking him. Now, make good use of this treasure."

She puts a small pencil in my hand. I press her hand warmly.

"Hey! You, there! Shut your mouths! March faster!" shout the guards.

My heart is so full of joy, their insults cannot touch me. I have a pencil! I want to shout for joy. I have paper! I have friends! I am going to write again.

The head count passes without incident. No one is punished today. I fly back into the barrack and gulp down my soup, all the time touching my pocket. It is still there. I slip into my bunk. I must write before they shut off the lights. My hands tremble as the pencil tip flows quickly over the brown pieces of paper, the paper collected so carefully by some of the girls in this barrack. I fold them smoothly to form a booklet, a friend.

I am in a daze. I stare at the written words. They are real. They look back at me. I read silently.

Camp Mittelsteine, Germany.
September 23, 1944
Riva Minska, Number 55082.

When my tormented heart can't take
    any more
The grief within rips it apart;
My tears flow freely—they can't be
    restrained
I reach for my notebook—my friend.
I speak to my friend of my sorrow
I share my anger, my pain.
I speak to my friend of tomorrow
Of a future we'll build once again!
The pillars I build for the future to
    come,
I knock down and build once again.

the cage

I share all my dreams, share my hopes
    with my friend
Share the pain that is filling my heart.

    I feel at ease now.

    "Tola," I whisper. "I have a pencil. I wrote a poem, on paper."

    Tola jumps up. "Girls! Riva has a pencil! She wrote a poem! Read, Riva! Read!" she shouts, excited.

    Heads poke out from the cubicles. Swollen red eyes stare at me, waiting. I feel so small. So scared now.

    I read slowly, my voice shaking. "'When my tormented heart can't take any more . . .'"

    Sobs fill the room

    "Riva, you speak for all of us," Tola says softly. "They cannot kill our spirit, our hunger to survive."

36

Some days I am filled with hope; others, despair takes over. I put my feelings on brown paper bags. I write poems.

On Sundays, if we are lucky and no punishments are given, I visit the girls in the other barracks. I read my poems. Some girls cry, some listen silently.

The cold, gray days of the season add to our hopelessness. Hungry, weak, beaten, we lie on the sacks of straw in our tiny cubicles. The days are so long. The work at the factory, the buckets of clay at the bunker, so fatiguing. They sap our last strength. It is hard to keep track of the days.

I lie staring at the yellowish rays thrown by the one small light bulb in the room. I feel only emptiness.

From the narrow opening of one of the bunks a head pokes out. Sara, one of the older girls, looks at the barbed-wire fence beyond the tiny barrack window. Softly she says, "Children, it is Hanukkah," more to herself than to anyone there.

the cage

Slowly the silence is broken. One by one, from the fifty wooden cubicles lining the walls of the barrack, heads slip out. Eyes open in bewilderment. "Hanukkah already?" Rosa says. "If I had my mama's latkes today . . ." And with tears in her voice, she adds, "If I had my mama today . . ."

Memories of Hanukkahs with mothers, fathers, sisters, brothers start coming back. Memories of another life. A life almost forgotten, of families sitting around tables, singing songs, sharing latkes, lighting candles, retelling the miracle of Hanukkah. The miracle of the brave Maccabees and their fight for the right to live as Jews. Their fight for religious freedom. Memories of Hanukkah plays, of Hanukkah games.

From the top bunk comes the start of a Hanukkah song:

Oh, you tiny candlelights
Stories you tell
Stories without end.

Slowly, softly, from all corners of the barrack, voices join in:

You tell of many bloody deeds
Of bravery and skill
Of wonders long ago.

Somehow strengthened, raising our voices
higher, we all sing:

When I see you twinkling bright
A dream arises brilliantly
Speaks an old dream.
Jews, there were battles you waged
Jews, there were victories
All so hard to believe.

Suddenly the guard's pounding at the door
brings us back to cruel reality. "What is going
on? Be still!" she shouts, banging with her rifle
at the door. "Stop, or I'll come in!"

We stop. A smile spreads over my face. The
emptiness is gone. I feel happy.

"We, too, have just won a victory," I whisper softly to the girl next to me.

Her hand touches mine. We press hands
silently.

37

A throbbing in my finger wakes me. I feel hot. My face is covered with perspiration. My right hand hurts.

Several days ago I cut my finger at work. The buckets have sharp edges. I have cut my hands before on the buckets. But this time my finger is swollen and throbbing. I must wait it out. I must not go to the doctor. She cannot help much.

"Who has any medical training among you?" the commandant called out one day during head count. No one answered. "Well, then," she said, her voice indifferent, her hand playing with her whip, "you will not have any doctor. It does not matter to me."

Still silence. "Girls, please. Don't be afraid. This is our only chance for medical help," Helen, the camp elder, said.

A girl of medium height, in her twenties, stepped forward. With her shaven head and wrapped in a shapeless dress, her wooden shoes clumsy on her feet, she did not look much like a doctor. "I am a medical student," she says softly. "I went to medical school in Budapest."

The commandant looked her over sharply, smiling ironically. "How many years of medical school do you have?"

"Two years, Madam Commandant."

"Well, then, you are the doctor."

And so the medical student from Budapest became a doctor. A doctor without medical tools, without medicines. A doctor who must report anyone who is sick more than three days.

When we take sick, we stay away from her tiny sickroom. We stay in the barrack, if possible. I close my eyes. I must hold out. I must not tell the doctor. It will heal. It is only a cut. My head feels so light. I am reaching for someone, but my hand feels so heavy. I moan.

"Riva! Riva! Open your eyes. Talk to me. What's wrong?"

Someone is touching my face. "She is burning up with fever. We must call the doctor." The voice sounds so far away.

"Let's put a cold compress to her head. We must wait until morning. We cannot leave the barrack now." I float away again. I float in an empty, endless space.

"Riva, how do you feel? Open your eyes." Our doctor is standing over me, gently touching my hot face.

"My hand hurts. I want to sleep." I close my eyes again.

"I know it hurts, child. You have an infection. You have fever. I must operate." She sounds worried. "You are lucky, Riva." She is trying to sound cheerful. "Just think. You are my first operation."

She turns to her nurse, a girl with training in first aid. "Let's get started."

I close my eyes. I am floating again in empty space.

"How is she doing?" The voice of the camp elder breaks through the haze. "It's several days since the surgery."

"The infection is spreading," I hear the doctor reply sadly.

"Is she dying?" the camp elder asks, her voice shaking. "What can you do, doctor?"

"I am helpless. She needs a hospital. A real doctor. She needs surgery. The blood poisoning is spreading so fast."

I lie still and listen. I am too tired to speak.

"Helen," the doctor says, "we must report the sick to the commandant."

There is silence. I feel a hand touching my face. "Riva, would you like some bread and jam?" the camp elder asks softly.

I open my eyes. I suddenly remember that when someone is dying, the camp elder offers her bread and jam, so she will not die hungry. "I am going to die." My voice sounds strange to me. "I am going to die. I do not want to die."

The doctor quickly takes my hand. "No, Riva. No. You are not going to die. I will find help."

The room looks blurry. I close my eyes and open them again. I see figures standing near the door, whispering. I strain my ears.

"Madam Commandant." It's the doctor's soft voice. "Riva is going to die without surgery."

My heart stops. They called the commandant. They had to report me. Now she is going to send me to the death camp, to Grossrosen.

"Well, what do you want me to do? We have no hospital."

"But, Madam Commandant," the doctor

pleads, "there is a hospital in the town of Glatz. Maybe you could send her there. Please, Madam Commandant."

"Are you crazy? Why should I send her anywhere?" the commandant shouts angrily.

The doctor speaks again, slowly, calmly, full of self-control: "Madam Commandant, I told you about Riva's poetry because I wanted you to see her as a person, not just as another inmate. I also wanted you to know what her poetry does for the morale of the other girls."

"So?"

"Is it not important that those girls be able to work for you? Madam Commandant, if those girls can no longer work, you will have no camp to lead. They will take us to Grossrosen. And you, too, will have a problem."

I hold my breath. I am sure the commandant will raise her whip at any moment and hit the doctor for daring to speak to her that way. The gentle, kind medical student from Budapest may pay with her life for her courage.

The doctor presses on without any sign of fear: "Madam Commandant, as long as the girls have a will to live, they can still work. The girls' morale is important. Riva is important for their morale. You must try to save her."

Again, silence. I can hardly breathe. The power of life and death is in the hands of the Nazi commandant, this cold, sadistic woman. What chance do I have?

"Well, well, doctor, you have nerve." The commandant's voice startles me. "I'll see about it. You have nerve."

I hear the door open and close.

"Doctor, you are incredible," says the camp elder.

"One has to do what is right," the doctor says quietly.

38

"Riva, wake up. Wake up, girl." The doctor's excited voice brings me out of my daze. "You are going to a hospital."

Her warm hands dress me quickly. She puts a coat with a yellow star around my shoulders, pins my number above the star. Then she puts a striped hat on my shaven head.

Suddenly the door to the sickroom opens. A woman in a crisp, brown Nazi uniform enters. She is about thirty years old, of medium height, with light brown hair brushed smoothly to the side under her brown uniform cap.

"Is she ready?" Her voice is impatient and hard.

"Yes, Madam Overseer," the camp elder replies quickly.

"Riva, Madam Overseer Lotta will take you to Glatz, to a hospital." Helen gives me a gentle squeeze. "Good luck, girl."

"You will be all right, Riva," the doctor says. "You will be all right."

The guard opens the door. "Let's go."

I follow her slowly, unsteady on my feet. Tear-filled eyes stare at me from all directions. "May God be with you," I hear someone call after me as we pass the open gate.

It feels so strange to walk on the pebbled road without the other prisoners. The guard walks a few feet behind me.

Silently we move forward toward the train station. My feet drag.

The snow-covered mountaintops glistening in the early morning sun, the crisp, fresh air, the peaceful stillness, all feel very strange, unreal. What am I doing here? I am so tired. I sit down in the middle of the road.

"What is the matter? What do you think you are doing?" The guard's angry voice startles me. She is standing over me, staring at me.

For a moment I had forgotten about her. "I cannot go on." I look straight at her. We gaze at each other silently, prisoner and guard.

Suddenly she reaches out to help me up. "What is your name?" Her voice has lost its anger. "Where are you from?"

"My name is Riva, Madam Overseer." My voice quivers. "I was born in Lodz, Poland."

the cage

"Oh, yes. I've heard of Lodz. It is a big city. We call it Litzmannstadt. Is that right?"

"Yes, Madam Overseer."

"Where is your family? Is anyone from your family here at the camp?"

"No, Madam Overseer. I am all alone here. My mother was taken away from the ghetto in 1942. My brothers and sisters . . . I do not know where they are now, if they are alive or . . ."

"That is bad. I am sorry."

She is human, I think. She did not hit me. She spoke to me. Under that brown Nazi uniform beats the heart of another human being.

We walk side by side now, slowly, silently.

At the station the train is waiting for its passengers. I stare at the men and women in their bright, warm coats entering the train. How clean. How peaceful it is at the station. The guard motions for me to follow as she enters the train.

Men, women, children—families are sitting together in the comfortable train, chatting, smiling, busy with their daily life. I stand in the corner, a pitiful creature wrapped in an old coat, marked with the Star of David, a number, a blue-and-white striped hat. The people in the

207

clean, cheerful train ignore me.

There are empty seats all around me, but I stand. The guard sits down, giving me a stern look that means, keep standing in the corner. I lean against the wall, not daring to move. What would happen, I wonder, if I had the nerve to ignore the guard's signal and sat down on the empty bench before me? I am too tired to think, too weak to take the chance. I wonder if the guard, who a while ago acted human, is also afraid to take the chance of letting me sit down.

We reach Glatz. I hold on to the wall to keep from falling. The train empties. We wait. The people pass me by, looking the other way. A little girl, about seven years old, blond pigtails dancing on the collar of her brightly colored coat, stops and stares at me. She whispers something to the finely dressed lady holding her hand. I hear woman say nervously, "Jew, Jew," as she pulls the child closer to her side and quickly leaves the train. I suddenly remember childhood stories of monsters and boogeymen. Am I their boogeyman?

We walk out from the station into the street through a side door. Rows of pretty houses line the streets. The guard signals me to get off the sidewalk and walk in the gutter. Jews are not permitted on the sidewalk.

I lower my head as I walk in the gutter. I feel the resentful glances of passersby. What is this bag of bones and rags doing in our clean, peaceful town?

We reach a hospital. The guard waits while I make my way slowly up the steps to the entrance. She enters, and I follow behind her. The hospital waiting area is filled with people sitting patiently in the sun-filled room, reading and talking. They look at me, puzzled.

My guard walks over to the reception desk. She speaks softly to the woman behind the desk, who is dressed in a nurse's uniform. "My prisoner needs medical help. She has blood poisoning. This is an emergency."

"Please wait," the nurse replies politely as she leaves the desk. She passes me by without looking at me. She returns after a short while. With her is a tall, blond man dressed in a white uniform. He introduces himself to the guard as the chief doctor.

"My prisoner must have medical attention." The guard repeats her request. "This is an emergency." Her voice is strong and self-assured.

The doctor looks at me icily. "My dear lady, we do not treat Jews. Please take her away from here." He turns and walks calmly away.

"I am an S.S. officer, doctor!" The guard raises her voice. The doctor turns. "I am an S.S. officer, and I have brought in a sick prisoner. She will die without medical care, doctor."

"My honorable S.S. officer, our boys on the front are also dying. We do not treat Jews. . . ."

Without another word, her face pale, eyes full of rage, the guard walks toward the door. I follow. The eyes of the silent onlookers chase me from this horrible place, where a doctor refuses help to a sick human being and not a word of protest is uttered.

I walk in the gutter again, the guard on the sidewalk. We reach another hospital. "Stay here, by the door," she says softly, while she enters the hospital.

My heart pounds each time someone stops to stare at me. My eyes glued to the hospital door, I wait. The guard finally appears in the doorway. I read the verdict in her crimson face. No help for Jews. She curses under her breath: "Idiots!"

the cage

We march on. My body is on fire, my mouth dry. I drag my wooden shoes in the gutter of this clean, quiet town.

We stop several times at clinics, only to be turned away. It is late in the day. I wish the guard would give up and take me back to the camp. I have to use the bathroom. I must hold back. I feel tears gliding over my face. I just want to sleep, sleep, sleep.

39

We are in front of yet another hospital. I wait outside alone. The staring people do not bother me anymore.

I sit down on the stone steps of the hospital entrance. I do not care what may happen. I only want to close my burning eyes.

Suddenly I hear the guard's voice. "Riva, get up, please."

I jump up, startled. I stare at her with dazed eyes. She called me by my name.

"Riva, I found a doctor. We must wait until she is finished with her patients. She will look at you then. We may go inside and wait." Her voice rings with triumph.

I follow her through the door, into the hospital. In the corner of the crowded waiting room there is an empty bench. She motions for me to sit. I sit at the edge of the bench, ready to jump at any moment, ready to be thrown out. But no one says anything. I slide back deeper into the wooden seat, breathing a little easier.

The guard takes a seat across from me and unbuttons her coat. She looks at me. Our eyes meet for a second. I see the sadness in hers. She lowers her head.

Most of the people around me are men in military uniforms. Some are without arms or legs. I feel sorry for them. I close my eyes. I am so tired. My head feels heavy as it wobbles back and forth. I am floating again. . . .

Suddenly the shriek of sirens fills the air. The people in the waiting room move quickly and in an orderly fashion toward a door marked SHELTER. The guard motions to me to follow her. We move with the others down the stairs to the bomb shelter and sit down.

Some people have turned already to their reading. A woman calmly takes out her knitting from a huge bag. "I always travel prepared for a long stay," she says to the young man sitting near her. He smiles back politely without saying a word. He is not wounded. He does not look sick. I wonder what he is doing here.

Some of the people glance in my direction and turn their heads quickly. I feel so strange, taking cover from planes whose arrival I welcome. I feel strange hiding with the Germans. At the factory we are left standing outside during air raids, while the Germans take cover. Here, if a bomb should hit, we will all die together.

"Ladies and gentlemen, the air raid is over. Thank you for your cooperation," says a voice over the loudspeaker. Everyone returns to the waiting room or to work.

Finally the waiting room is empty. From somewhere a blond woman in her forties walks over to the guard. They both look at me as they speak. The woman, dressed in a white uniform, takes my hand and leads me to a small examination room.

"Thank you for seeing us, doctor," the guard says, looking at the woman warmly. "I could not give up."

"I am sorry I had to make you wait so long. You understand . . . I must treat our people first. And then the air raid . . .":

The doctor speaks to the guard while gently helping me up on the examination table. Her warm hands feel soothing as she touches my forehead. She holds my throbbing hand.

"This is bad, very bad. I must operate right here, now. We must not call too much attention to this patient." She takes a deep breath.

"There are some who would resent her being here."

Am I dreaming? The doctor's voice sounds so far away. I am somewhere in space, floating, floating.

"Riva. Wake up, little one." Someone is shaking me. "We must leave."

I keep my eyes closed. It is so peaceful here. I do not want to leave.

"We must leave, Riva." The guard helps me up.

"Careful. Don't let her fall. She is still dizzy," the doctor says while helping me dress. She walks us to the hospital door.

"Thank you, doctor," I whisper. She smiles sadly.

The streets are dark now. The streetlamps along the sidewalks glow in the darkness. I walk in the gutter again. Like a drunk, I sway from side to side. People stop to stare. I ignore them.

I feel my knees buckling. I am about to fall in the gutter. A hand grabs me just in time and holds me up. "Riva, you must hold on. I cannot hold you," the guard says. She looks around. People stare at the woman in a Nazi uniform holding up a half-dead Jew.

She walks behind me now, gently pushing me forward.

The train has few riders. I stand in the corner. My feet cannot hold me up. I lower myself to the floor and sit, closing my eyes. I float between dream and reality. Mama is looking down at me, her eyes so loving. She keeps on looking at me but does not speak. Strange people keep walking by. Their angry eyes scare me. They shout at me, reaching out to grab me.

Someone is shaking me by my shoulders. "Riva, get up. We are home."

I open my eyes, confused. I whisper: "Home? Home?"

Lotta, the guard, is helping me up. The train is empty. The conductor stands by the door. He says something to the guard. She walks me toward the back of the station.

I feel hands lifting me up and gently lowering me into something. "Riva. Thank God, you are alive!" someone says in Yiddish. I open my eyes slowly. My eyelids feel so heavy.

"Where am I?"

"You are back in Mittelsteine. We have the wagon. We are taking you back to camp. Sleep. Sleep."

the cage

The girls pull the wagon along the pebbled road.

"Careful. Careful. Go slowly," the guard says. "Take her home slowly."

The girls are taking me home—back to the cage.

40

I open my eyes. Blurred faces look down at me.

"Riva, how are you feeling?" asks the camp doctor. "How are you feeling?" She touches me gently.

"My hand . . . it hurts. I am so thirsty."

"I know, child." She moistens my lips with water. "We have to take you back to the hospital in Glatz. The doctor there wants to see you."

"But I just came back. I am so tired." It takes so much effort to speak.

"You came back several days ago." She wipes my forehead with a wet cloth. It feels good.

"I want to sleep. Please . . ."

"No, dear girl. We must get you dressed. We have to leave soon. I am going with you. Lotta asked me to go, to help you walk. She told me how you staggered all the way home."

I hear the tears in her voice. Is she crying for me? Am I dying?

The doctor holds me up as we walk

through the beautiful mountainside. The cold air feels refreshing on my hot face. The guard walks in front of us, stopping each time we lag behind. She waits silently for us to catch up with her.

We reach the station as if in a dream, a dream I have lived through before. I stand in the corner of the train. My head rests heavily on the doctor's arm. She caresses my head and holds on to the wall to keep us both from falling. The guard sits on the bench, watching us. She turns her face toward the window.

We reach Glatz. The camp doctor and I step into the gutter. I look at her with feverish eyes. She walks proudly, holding her head high, hugging me close to her.

My eyes rest on the number and the yellow star on her coat. I feel a huge lump in my throat. "Doctor, I'm sorry. I'm sorry you have to march like this, in the gutter, with them staring at us. I'm sorry you have to suffer this humiliation because of me. You are such a special person."

"Riva," she says, lifting my chin high, "we are all special. Hold your head proudly. Let those who put us in the gutter feel shame, not us." She presses my hand warmly. "We are special, Riva. We are better. We can still feel."

We reach the hospital. It is still early in the morning. The doctor I remember bending over me is waiting for us. She ushers us into an examination room. I sit down. The camp doctor and the guard stand by my side.

"How is she doing?" the doctor asks the guard.

"She is still running a high fever, doctor," the camp doctor speaks up. The doctor looks at her silently, then at the guard.

"Forgive me. This is the camp doctor. I asked her to come, to help the girl."

"Good. Very good." She pauses, looking at the young woman in an old coat, marked with a yellow star and a number. "How is she doing, doctor?"

"She is in a lot of pain, doctor."

Their eyes meet silently. The doctor cuts the bandage. I watch her face, holding my breath. The gauze is sticking to the wound. I bit my lips.

"She is a brave girl, sitting so still. This is very painful."

The doctor speaks to the camp doctor and

the guard as if I were not there. She speaks German. The last piece of dressing is off. The guard turns her face away.

I watch the doctor's eyes. They are full of distress.

"Oh, my, we still have a problem." She turns to the camp doctor. "I'll clean it out and put on a fresh dressing. The poison is still spreading up her hand." She sighs. "We'll wait a few more days. Then bring her back." She stops, taking a deep breath. "If it does not improve, I will have to amputate her arm."

"Oh, God!" the camp doctor cries out.

I feel the chair sliding out from under me. I gasp for air. My eyes close.

"Riva! Riva! Open your eyes." The camp doctor holds something under my nose. It smells strong. "Come on, child, don't faint."

I open my eyes slowly, looking straight into the doctor's horror-stricken face. "I am sorry. I did not know she understood German."

Tears flow silently down my face. She wipes them gently.

We march back to the train. The sun is strong, but I feel only darkness around me.

"Doctor." I find it hard to speak. "Doctor,

you must make me a promise."

She looks at me.

"You must promise . . . if the infection is not better . . . you will not let them amputate." I stop. "They will not need me with one arm. I'll die either way. Please, don't let them cut off my arm. Promise."

She pulls me closer to her.

"Doctor, when they put me to sleep I will be helpless. I do not want to wake up with one arm. You must promise you will not let her do it. Please. Promise."

"Riva, the surgery may save your life," she says meekly.

"You know it will not save me. Let me die of the poisoning."

I see the pain in her face. "I promise," she says. "I promise."

41

On my third trip to the hospital, the doctor finds that the poison has stopped spreading. Thank God. There will be no amputation.

Slowly my hand shows improvement. The incision reaches from my wrist to the tip of my second finger, as if my hand had been cut into two pieces and then sewn together again. The finger is stiff.

"Well, Riva, a stiff finger is better than no hand." The camp doctor smiles sadly as she changes the bandages on my hand. "Just think, you will take out with you from this hell a reminder that someone cared if you lived or died."

She looks around at the patients on the sacks of straw. "I will remember my internship here. And you, my first surgery." She sighs a deep, heavy sigh. "We must do the best we can—and live."

"If I could write again, I would feel more alive." I stare at my bandaged right hand.

"What is the use? I am right-handed."

The doctor stops for a moment. She puts my hand gently down on the blanket and walks briskly toward the little room she shares with the nurse and the camp elder. My eyes follow her through the open door. I see her search for something in a small box under her bunk. She takes something from the box and returns, smiling.

In her hand she carries a pencil and a piece of paper. Gently she props me up against the wall behind the bunk and sits down near me. "Give me your left hand, Riva."

"What are you going to do, doctor?" I ask, agitated.

"Riva. Trust me, child. God gave you two hands, right? I will teach you to use your left hand."

She puts the small pencil in my hand and slowly guides my fingers over the paper. It feels clumsy but good. I smile as I see on the paper the shapes I form with my left hand.

"See, Riva? Soon you will learn to form letters with your left hand. So what if they don't look perfect."

She spends every free moment with me,

helping me exercise my fingers, encouraging me while guiding my hand over the paper. "Riva, you are doing better every day," she says happily.

Slowly words take shape on the paper she brings me. I write again. I hear the whistle outside my little world calling for head count. I hear the sound of the whip, the shouts. I cover my ears. I am lucky. I am in the sickroom, and I write.

Each evening lines form in front of the sickroom, girls waiting for first aid. I hear their voices, weak and worn. I see the sorrow, the helplessness in the doctor's eyes when she comes late in the evening to look at the lucky ones, the ones who got to be admitted for the night. Gently she touches my hair when she sees me write. "We must never give up, girls. We must never give up."

The goddess of the sick. I write these words on the paper.

"Doctor, this is for you." I hand her a piece of paper with an awkward smile.

"Riva, I cannot read Yiddish. Would you please read it to me." She sits on the edge of the bunk, waiting.

I feel myself blush as I read:

"The goddess of the sick.
We have a sickroom in this place
you're lucky to get into
sad when you must leave.
Our doctor, our goddess
is always nearby
to chase the pain and sorrow
with words of love
with words of hope
hope for a better tomorrow.
Her daily care: pills of faith
a smile
a touch of her hand
tales
tales of the life that waits.
We gain strength from her strength
gain hope from her hope
warmed by the rays of her love."

A dark shadow covers her face. "Riva, I am
no goddess. I am Anna, a medical student from
Budapest, and very, very human."

She sighs. "Love is not always enough," she
says. "Did you know that I have a husband?" I

gaze at her, surprised. "Do you know where my husband is?" She does not wait for my reply. "No, he is not in a concentration camp like you and me. He is not a Jew. He is a young doctor I met in medical school. We were married for a short time only, a very short time. The Nazis put him in an army uniform and sent him away to heal the killers of my people. He is free; I am here. His family is alive; mine was murdered in Auschwitz." She stops for a moment. "I still love him, but if I survive I will never go back to him. The barbed wire will always be between us. Even love will not—"

"I am sorry, doctor. I did not mean to—"

She squeezes my hand and walks quickly to her room, closing the door behind her.

42

"Riva, they are closing the factory for the Christmas holiday," Helen, the camp elder, says, sitting down on my bunk heavily. "The guards will be bored, so the commandant wants us to put on a show. We must give them some amusement, or they will find their amusement in the whip."

She turns to the doctor, who is bathing my hand in a small basin. "Can Riva leave the sickroom? Can she come and read some of her poems?"

"I don't know. Riva is still weak. I'm afraid the commandant may have her sent back to the factory if she sees her out of bed." She hesitates for a moment. "Well, she has already told me that I am keeping Riva here much too long. But I don't know if we should take the chance. . . ."

My eyes wander from one to the other. The doctor is trying to protect me; the camp elder trying to do what is best for all. I feel torn. I want to stay here in safety as long as possible.

Still, if I can help calm the beasts for a while, I must. "I will be strong, doctor. I will be part of the show. We must do the best we can, you always say."

She smiles. "The girls will be happy to see you."

Helen puts her hand on my shoulder. "Thank you, Riva." She leaves to search for more talent for the command performance.

The day arrives. My heart pounds as I walk into the barrack reserved for the show. The doctor holds her arm around me to help me walk. Four hundred voices cheer. I won a battle for life. They were all part of my struggle. They prayed for me. I won. They won.

The commandant enters, followed by her guards. She looks around, her eyes angry, as always, then motions to the camp elder to take over.

We are ordered to sit. Helen stands on the platform built for this occasion and begins the program by wishing the commandant and her gang a Merry Christmas. Then, one by one, the girls walk up to the platform to show off their talent in ballet, poetry, song. I sit enchanted. So much talent is still alive in those dried-out young bodies. They dance and sing for their captors, but it seems to me they are at this moment in a world of their own, a world of beauty. I glance quickly at the commandant and the guards. They look amazed.

Karola steps up on the platform. My heart pounds. I know the poem she is going to recite, "Bread Given Back." The poem tells of a regime that brings slavery and misery to a people and of a new regime that pays back the oppressor with the same misery it caused.

Karola recites the poem in Yiddish. Yiddish sounds a lot like German. If the Nazis should understand the message . . . . A chill goes through my body as I listen to Karola finish in a strong, determined voice.

The commandant bends over to the guard at her side. They whisper. The commandant shrugs her shoulders. I take a deep breath. They ignore the message.

Now it is my turn. To reach the platform I have to pass the commandant. I look the other way. I feel her staring at me as the doctor helps me onto the platform.

"Is that the one with the blood poisoning,

doctor?" she says, surprised.

"Yes, Madam Commandant. I took her out for the first time today."

I feel the commandant's eyes piercing me. I avoid her gaze. Looking straight at the girls in front of me, I, too recite in Yiddish:

"A message for Mama.
Blue little clouds, floating so free
Won't you please carry a message for me
if on your journey you should
    happen to see
my mother."

My voice cracks. My personal message to Mama is the message of the four hundred Nazi victims in this camp to four hundred mothers crying for their children. My voice becomes stronger.

"Tired, weary, left all alone
torn from her children
filled with sorrow and pain.
Please, gently touch her
please, gently kiss her
bring her my love.

Tell how I miss her.
Feel her pain, feel her sorrow
please tell her, my friends,
she must live for tomorrow!
If you see her tears,
please wipe them
tell her
soon, soon will come the day
when together again
together again we will be.
A mother, her children—a family
all free!
Mama, dear Mama,
please whisper for me
today will vanish—believe.
Soon your empty arms
your children will fill
the sorrow will turn to joy.
Tomorrow is near
dear Mama, please live!
Be strong
we'll weather this storm.
We'll find you, dear Mama
please, do not despair
we will live!
We will live to be free!"

the cage

I feel my knees bending. I feel hands grabbing me. Someone is carrying me.

I open my eyes slowly. I am back in the sickroom. Beside me sits the doctor. "Welcome back, Riva. You made me a bit nervous. You passed out."

She caresses my head softly. "I should have kept you here to begin with. You are still too weak and—" She stops suddenly, her eyes in the doorway. I look up. Standing there in her brown Nazi uniform, club in hand, is the commandant.

I lower my eyes. She has come to punish me for my poetry. She is going to send me away. I look at the doctor. She still holds her hand on my head, as if to protect me.

"Leave us, doctor," the commandant orders. The doctor remains standing by my side, her eyes angry and defiant.

"Leave us, please." The commandant's voice is softer now. The doctor moves slowly toward the door.

My heart beats wildly as I watch her leave the room. I am all alone now. All alone with this beast who takes pleasure in punishing her helpless victims.

Suddenly she sits down at the edge of my bunk, her eyes studying my face intently. I lie still.

She puts her hand in the pocket of her Nazi uniform and pulls out a small notebook. She tosses it onto my blanket. I remain still. She does not take her eyes off my face as she puts her hand back into her pocket. "You do not have to hide your poetry," she says. "I was sure that we killed all your emotions, that all you can feel is hunger, all you can think of is bread." She stops, looking away. "Your poems are full of hope, of love. You still feel. You still dream. You yearn for your mother. You reminded me that I, too, have a mother."

She stands up and leaves the room without looking at me.

I pick up the notebook with shaking hands. This did not really happen. I must be dreaming. There is something human in that woman, something that can be moved by a poem. I touch the small notebook. It is real. I am not dreaming. It is real. It is real.

43

It is January 19, 1945. I am writing a poem when the doctor enters the sickroom. She stands by the door and waits. I feel her looking at me as I write. I look up and meet her worried eyes. She sits down at the edge of my bunk, taking my hand in hers. "Riva," she says, "you are going to the factory tomorrow. You have to. The commandant is expecting the inspector soon."

"What will they do with me? I cannot work in the factory. I can't see. I cannot work in the bunker. I can't use my hand."

"Riva, you will be strong." She turns abruptly and walks out, closing the door to the tiny room behind her.

I lie on the straw, waiting restlessly for the shrill sound of the wake-up whistle, for five o'clock in the morning. As I walk out of the sickroom, the icy air hits my face. My legs move unsteadily toward the lines of girls standing in the field. It is time for head count.

I see the fearful eyes of the frail girls before

me. "Good luck," someone whispers. "Good luck, Riva."

"Silence." A guard raises her whip.

The commandant arrives, her dog at her side. She whispers something to one of the guards and motions to the camp elder to give the order to march.

It has been almost three months since I last marched on these roads. I have forgotten the long, hard march to the factory, the sounds of the whips, the shrieks of the guards. I drag my wooden shoes heavily on the snow-covered road. My feet feel as if they, too, were wooden.

"March! March! Do not fall behind," a guard shouts.

I speed up. "Give me your hand. You will walk faster if you hold on to me." I take the hand of the ragged shadow marching near me and walk.

We reach the factory. The girls who work in the factory line up at one side of the field, the girls who work at the bunker at the other. I move toward the girls going to the bunker.

"Hey, you! Come here," a guard calls, pointing at me. She looks at me with disdain. "Wait here." Her voice is cold and harsh. The girls march off to work. Will I see them again?

"Let's go. Stop dreaming. March!" The guard moves forward with big strides. I try to keep up with her and find myself running.

We stop in front of a small, white building. I am out of breath. The front door is open. We enter a long, narrow hall. Some of the doors along the wall are open, and I see bathtubs and toilets. The last door at the end of the hall has a sign that reads FIRST AID.

I lean against the wall. The guard stares at me. "Now, now. Don't you faint on me. Doctor!" she calls nervously.

The door opens. A tall woman in a white uniform rushes toward me. She guides me toward the room. "Sit down, girl." She helps me into a chair. "Take off your coat." She hands me a glass of water. "Drink. You will be all right." She speaks German with a heavy Russian accent. Her voice is strained.

"Is this the one?" she asks the guard. Her Russian accent puzzles me.

"This is the one, doctor. I will call for her when it is time."

I listen to the strange exchange of words. Time for what?

The guard leaves. I stare at the woman before me. She takes my hand. "Poor girl," she says. She clears her throat. "You will be fine. I am Katia. I am the doctor here. I give first aid to the workers." Her light brown hair pulled toward the back of her head adds gentleness to her young face. Her warm voice, her Russian accent soothe me. "You will help wash, sterilize, and reroll the bandages to be reused." She sighs. "And you will wash the bathtubs and toilets out there. The German workers use them."

She still holds my hand. "You are very lucky. The Nazi commandant from your camp came here last week. She asked if I could find work for you here. It is better than the factory or the bunker." She studies the long, red scar on my hand. "She told me about the blood poisoning. You are lucky. You are very lucky.

"I am Russian. My husband is also Russian, of German ancestors. When the Germans took Russia, they told him he is a German and sent him to the front. I followed to be as close to him as possible. I have not heard from him for a long time now." She sighs a painful sigh. "Where are you from, child? What is your name?"

"My name is Riva Minska. I was born in Lodz, Poland."

"Oh, yes, yes. I was in Poland awhile. Yes, yes . . . someday you will go back home, but I will never go home. I have my family in Russia. I hope they are alive. I can never go back to Russia. I left Russia. I followed my husband. I can never go home."

"Doctor, thank you for letting me work here." My voice breaks.

"Oh, child, I don't feel much like a doctor. I feel more like a prisoner. Please call me Katia. I like to hear my Russian name."

She puts a basket with clean bandages before me. "Roll them up slowly. Take your time. There is no guard here." She smiles. "If I see a guard, I'll let you know. We will be friends."

44

"Riva, it is good to see you." The girls of Barrack Two greet me with open arms.

"It was so depressing to look at your empty bunk." Tola hugs me close to her, like a mother welcoming her long-lost child.

"We missed you. Where did they take you today? We looked for you."

"My heart stopped beating when they ordered you to remain standing alone on the field." Karola puts her arms around me. "It is good to have you back, Riva."

I share the details of my day with my fifty roommates and crawl into my old bunk. It feels strange being back here. The wood from the bunk above me looks as if it will fall down on my head any moment. In the sickroom I had no bunk above or below me.

The doctor and the camp elder come to check on me. "I was so worried about you, Riva," the doctor says. "I did not know what they were planning to do. The commandant is very unpredictable. I'm glad you're all right." She smiles. "Remember, you are still my patient. After work, come have me look at you."

I lie on the straw, thinking about the Nazi commandant. How can she act human to one person and be such an ugly beast to others? I wish she would be more human to all.

But wishing does not make it so. The whip continues to fall on the girls' backs. Cursed, beaten, we march daily to the factory and back to the cage, urged on by the angry guards. The snow-covered roads make the long march even harder. The canvas on my shoes is coming off. The wooden bottoms allow the snow to glide freely in my shoes.

Katia looks at my half-frozen feet with pity and anger. She massages my frozen toes and ties my shoes together with old bandages to hold them on my feet. She curses under her breath. "Nazi murderers."

Some days Katia brings warm mashed potatoes, cooked vegetables, or bread hidden in her coat pockets. "Eat, child, eat." She watches with pleasure as I swallow the food quickly. She knows it will mean trouble for her if I am caught, but she still takes the chance.

"How long has it been since you had a warm bath?" She stands in the doorway of the bathroom, watching me scrub the tub a German woman has just used.

"How long, Riva, dear? How long?" I am trying hard to remember. It has been so long. "I'm not sure, Katia. In the ghetto we had hardly enough wood to keep warm. Once a week we warmed up some water, put it in a basin, and my brothers and I would wash in it." My voice breaks. I see the gentle young faces before me. I hear them urging me: *You go first, Riva. Girls need warm water for their hair. Girls must look pretty even in the ghetto.*

She waits, silently watching as I wipe the tears from my face. I swallow hard. "In the camps, Katia, we use cold water in a basin and then wash our underwear and dress in the same water. A warm bath? I forget what it is like."

She moves quickly toward the bathtub, opens the faucet, and begins to fill the tub. "Now, then, it is time for you to have a warm bath. I will stand guard outside."

She leaves the room, leaving me standing in

a daze. Nervously I slip out of my clothes and slide slowly into the warm water, too frightened to enjoy the luxurious gift.

I must wash up quickly, before someone comes and finds me here. If they should catch me in the bathtub, Katia will be in a lot of trouble, and I—I will surely be punished.

Katia knocks softly on the door. I hold my breath. "It is all right, Riva. No one is coming. I want to remind you to wash your hair, too."

I take a deep breath. I am still safe. I dip my head into the warm water. What delight. How wonderful it feels to wash my hair in warm water. How much we take for granted. I hurry out of the tub. I must not get Katia into trouble. Smiling, I stand before Katia with a towel around my wet hair. Her face glows with joy. "We did it, Riva! You look so fresh, so clean, so new. We will do this again." There is a note of mischief and defiance in her voice. "We will do it again."

I smile as I rub my wet hair with the towel. "Thank you, dear Katia. I am—" I stop, frozen with fear. Staring straight at me from the front entrance is a Nazi guard. Her eyes flash angrily.

"What is going on here? What is the meaning of this, doctor?"

"The meaning of what, Madam Overseer?" Katia's voice is calm and strong.

"Why is this prisoner wearing a towel?" She walks over and pulls the towel from my head. "Why is her hair wet, doctor?"

Katia remains calm. "This girl slipped in the tub while cleaning. She got all wet. Well, she has to dry off, Madam Overseer."

"She slipped! Ha!" The guard keeps her cold gaze on the doctor's face.

"Yes, Madam Overseer," Katia replies.

"Well, see to it that it does not happen again." The guard turns to me. "Don't be such a clumsy oaf." She walks out, the sound of her boots echoing loudly in the silence of the room.

"We will do it again," Katia whispers softly. "We will do it again."

Daily, Katia brings the latest news, which I eagerly await. "They are doing badly, Riva. They are taking a beating on all fronts. Soon it will be over. You'll see."

There is joy and sadness in her voice. "My people, the Russians, are coming closer. But I cannot be here when they come. To them I am a traitor."

"No, Katia, dear. You are not a traitor. You

left your family, your home, to be with your husband. They cannot punish you for that."

She smiles sadly. "I wish you were right. I do not even know where my husband is. I will search for him. But I will never go home again. They will not forgive me."

I feel so sorry for Katia. What a terrible price to pay for loving her husband. Never to see her family again. Tears fill my eyes. Family. Where is mine? Will I ever find them?

Katia hugs me close, wiping the tears from my face.

45

"Out! Out! Everyone, out!" The guards run from barrack to barrack, banging on the doors with their clubs. "Line up! Quickly! Quickly!"

We jump out from the bunks. It is still too early for work. We dress quickly, asking one another, What are they up to now?

The door opens. The camp elder, pale and nervous, stands in the doorway. Her eyes are red and frightened.

"Girls, take your belongings. They are moving us."

"Where are we going? What are they going to do with us? What did they tell you?"

"I do not know, girls. I do not know what they are going to do. Hurry. They are all in an uproar. Something is happening. Girls, please hurry. Let's not give them any reason for punishment."

"Since when do they need a reason?" one of the girls calls boldly.

Helen lowers her head. "No, they do not

need a reason, but if we follow their orders, maybe . . ." She turns and walks out.

I take my notebook of poems, my friend, my only belonging. I put it inside my blouse, close to me. I must protect it.

We line up. The commandant walks into the camp, her whip swishing loudly as she stops in front of us.

"Well, ladies," she says. "I saw your joy when you heard the bombs. Yes, we have some problems at the moment, but I assure you, ladies, no matter how badly things go for us, you will never live to be freed." She stops, studying the effect of her words. "Before we die—one minute before we die—you will die first."

We gasp with horror. From the open gates trucks enter the camp. The commandant waits for the trucks to line up. "Now, my dear ladies, I am sure next time you hear bombs you will remember my message. And in case you did not hear me, I repeat, you will not live to be freed!"

She turns to the guards. "Put them on the trucks. Take them to the other camps!"

Camps. Camps. The word penetrates my numbness. Camps. We are being sent to several different places. Separated. "Karola." I swallow the lump in my throat. "Karola, let's stay together. No matter what, let's stay together." I look at my friend, and I hear her mother's voice as we enter the cattle cars. *Stay together, children. Stay together, children.*

Karola presses my hand in silent agreement. Tola is in the line in front of us. I bend toward her. "Stay with us. Stay with us." She nods her head, her eyes fixed on the trucks.

"Forward, march! The first two rows, forward. Into the wagons!" The girls in the first rows move forward and climb into the waiting wagons.

"Be strong, my friends," one of the girls calls. The sound of the whip hisses through the air and falls on her head. She curls up in pain. The truck moves out.

"Next two rows, forward, march!" Tola's row moves forward. Karola and I move quickly into her group. We must stay together. The guards count heads as the trucks are loaded with their human cargo. Tola climbs into the truck. I move forward. "Stop, you idiot!" the guard calls, pushing me back. "Next truck. This truck is full."

the cage

Panic grips me. They are separating us. I move toward the truck when the guard turns her eyes. She grabs me suddenly, twisting my head toward her. "I told you, next truck, you cow!" She pushes me away.

Karola holds me up and helps me into the next truck. "Riva, are you all right? Did she hurt you?" she whispers.

"Karola, they are separating us again. First they took Mama. Then your mother. Our brothers. Now our friend." I put my head on Karola's shoulder. She puts her arm around me.

The trucks move forward, rushing, carrying us to the unknown. We search frantically for clues to our destination. From the back of the truck comes the mournful lament of a girl who was separated from her sister. "Where are you, sister, dear? Where are you?"

Along the road we see pretty, well-kept houses, people going about their daily routines. Some glance at the famished, horrified passengers of the trucks and turn their heads. Others ignore us.

My heart pounds when I see the barbed wire of our new cage. What is waiting for us behind that wire? I wonder, What do the people in their cozy little homes on this road feel? They see the trucks arriving. They see the human cargo. They must know what goes on behind that fence. Don't they care?

The gates open. Before us many barracks are spread about a large field. The truck stops in front of a long, low barrack. "Everyone, out!" I look for smoke, for chimneys. The sky is clear. I take a deep breath. The air is clean. No smoke.

The guards raise their arms in Nazi salute as a young man in a brown Nazi uniform approaches our group. We stand frozen in place. He returns their salute while his cold, hard eyes move quickly over his new shipment. "So this is my new labor force? These dried-up bones?" He swishes his whip angrily. "You are here to dig trenches. If you are lazy or sick. . . ." He cracks his whip and walks off.

The guards order us into the barrack, our new home. Rows and rows of wooden bunks reach to the ceiling. Eyes, wretched, dejected, stare at the new victims, searching for a familiar face.

"Riva! Riva! Thank God!" A shout of joy, and bony arms encircle my shaking body and keep me from falling. Tola's soft, brown eyes look at me in disbelief. "I thought we would never see each other again. Thank God we are still together. I don't know where the others were sent. This camp is Grafenort. In German it means a place for nobles."

She touches my face gently. "We are nobles, broken in body but still alive. And we are still together."

46

Knee-deep in mud, I dig the shovel into the earth, lift the heavy load, and throw dirt over the side. The guards, their rifles pointed at us, urge us on with shouts and curses. "Faster! Move! Move, cursed Jew."

What irony: the Nazi victims digging ditches for the Nazis so they can resist our liberators. I wonder how many people will die here. How many of my friends will find their graves here?

The first signs of spring are in the air. Life is renewing itself. Birds sing, early spring flowers bloom while death is staring at us. I see the ditches flowing with young blood. I put the shovel deep into the ground in silent protest, ignoring the guard above me. "Are you crazy? Why are you staring at me with your crazy eyes?" he asks. He lowers the rifle on my head. "You *are* crazy."

I hear the screams around me as I slip into the soft mud. "What do you think you are doing, Riva?" One of the girls helps me up, wiping my face with her coat. "We are all alone here, Riva. All alone, forgotten by the world, at the mercy of murderers."

I swallow my tears and dig again.

The sound of bombs far away brings hope and fear. "The bombs do not mean liberation," the guards remind us daily. "The day before we die, all of you will die first. The bombs do not mean the end of Germany; they mean the end of the Jews."

Their rifle butts dance over our shoulders. "The end is coming for you, Jews."

I hear Mama's voice: *As long as there is life, there is hope. As long as there is life . . .*

My arms ache. Sweat pours from my face as I lift the heavy dirt. "You are digging your own grave," I mumble slowly, "your own grave. As long as there is life, there is hope." Hope . . . hope . . . hope . . .

Karola's voice brings me back to reality. "Riva, do you know what date it is?"

I stare at her. "What difference does it make? For us, each day is the same."

She smiles sadly. "Riva, it is May 3, 1945— your birthday." She throws a kiss in my direction. "It is your birthday, and look where you celebrate your birthday—in a ditch. Maybe next year, if we survive."

"We must survive, Karola. We must survive." I raise my voice. "We must hope. As long as there is life, there is hope."

The guard, his face covered with a sarcastic smirk, pokes me with his rifle butt. "This is your last birthday, Jew. By next year you will all be dead."

47

May 5. It is very early in the morning. "Out! Out! Line up!" Heads are counted. The camp commandant whispers something to one of the guards and then gives the order: "Forward, march!"

We leave the camp. Outside the cage the white, serene homes look like something from a beautiful picture postcard. I wonder, Does our daily march, the sound of our wooden shoes on the pebble road, ever disturb the sleep of the people who live inside? Do they wonder, as they drink their hot morning coffee, where those skeletons are taken twice a day?

"Are you in another world again?" I hear someone alongside me whisper. "Did you notice, this is not the same road we turn onto each day. There is something going on. I can feel it." I look around me. There are more guards here today. Most of them are riding their bicycles, shouting at us, cursing us, swinging their clubs along the way. The road does not look the same. There are stretches of woods in the distance.

"Well, maybe they have enough ditches. They've found something new for us to do. Don't worry." I try to convince myself that there is nothing to panic about.

"Did you see how nervous they are today?" someone else whispers behind me.

"I think they are finished," another voice whispers. "Will they—" She too, is afraid to say what she is thinking.

The same fear, the same horrible thoughts fill each one of us.

The woods are getting closer. My heart beats like a drum, pounding, pounding, pounding. If we should die here, will anyone remember us? Will anyone tell our story? I press my notebook close to me.

I hear prayers. I join in silently.

The woods are before us. The first rows are about to enter.

"Halt! Stop!" A soldier speeding by on a motorcycle calls to the guards in front of the marching columns. "Halt! Halt!" he calls frantically. The guards stop. We stop.

In the silence the soldier's agitated outcry

echoes loudly and clearly: "The Russians are behind us! The Russians are behind us!" The guards stay frozen for a moment. Then, crazed by the news, they take off, leaving us standing on the road, bewildered.

We do not move. "Stand still, girls," someone says. "This may be a trick. Do not move. They may be waiting for us to start running. Then they will start to shoot." We stare at one another. No one moves.

Suddenly one girl shouts: "Girls, it is not a trick. I heard the guards. Death was waiting for us in the woods." She sobs. "They had orders to kill us all. One of the guards shouted, 'We must follow orders, we must follow orders, we cannot leave yet!' 'Forget about the Jews. Run, save your own life,' another shouted back. Girls! Girls, we are free! Free!"

Silence hangs frozen in the air. Hysterical cries break the stillness. "Oh, dear God! They were going to do what they said they would. They were going to kill us."

Tears fall freely over my sunken cheeks. As long as there is life, there is hope. We turn away from the woods. But we are still not free. We have nowhere to go. In back of us are the woods, our mass grave. Before us the road leads to the cage.

"Where do we go? Where do we run to?" Someone voices my thoughts.

"Let's knock on the doors of the homes here and ask for help," another voice calls.

Some girls walk slowly toward them and knock, first softly, then louder and louder. No one answers. No one opens the door. They are hiding from us.

Slowly we drag ourselves back, back to the open gates of the cage.

"Are we safe here?"

"Where can we go?"

"No one will help us."

"We have no place to go."

"Let's stay here and wait."

We lie on the sacks of straw, too weak, too numb to move. The gates are open, but no one leaves. We wait. If our liberators come, we will be here waiting for them.

May 7, 1945. He enters the gates of the cage like a prince in a fairy tale, a Russian officer on a white horse. Russian soldiers, tired, muddy, follow him slowly. We gather around them. They stare at us as if seeing ghosts coming out of a grave. The officer, a middle-aged man, gets off his horse slowly. Hands reach out to touch him. Is he real?

He seems shocked as the bony, out-stretched hands touch him. His voice quivers. He speaks Yiddish. "Are there Jews here?" he asks.

"Yes! Yes! We are Jews! We are still alive!"

Tears fall freely over his weatherbeaten face. "You are the first Jews we have found still alive." His voice breaks. "We liberated several concentration camps and found only ashes, dead bodies. I am a Jew. I had given up hope of finding any of my people alive. You are the first . . . the first. . . ."

We are all sobbing. "What happened to our families? Did they—"

He shakes his head sadly. "So many . . . so many . . . so many dead . . . so many murdered . . . so many murdered . . . Thank God I have found some of my people alive." He covers his face with his hands, and a wretched cry rips through the air.

48

"Could it happen here, Mommy? Could it happen again?" Nancy, my daughter, asks. I read the fear, the confusion written over her young face.

I take a deep breath. "If we forget the past, it could happen again. We must learn from these horrors. We must learn what happens when people remain silent while others are persecuted." I feel the sharp pain of remembering. "We must learn, my child, not to ignore the ugly signs, the danger signs, as my family—as the people of my generation—did."

She puts her arms around me. "After the Russians freed you, did you ever go back to Lodz to search for your family?"

"Yes. It was a long and hard journey, but I made my way back to Lodz. I still hoped to find Mama, Motele, Moishele. I survived, why shouldn't they? I was the sickly one. Motele, Moishele, they were the strong ones. I still hoped.

the cage

"A Polish woman stood in the doorway of my old home. 'What do you want? What are you looking for?'

"'I—I came—' I stammered. 'I am back from the camps. I lived here before they took us away.'

"Through the partially open door, our furniture stared back at me, as if demanding, Where are they? Why did you come back alone? I felt guilty, guilty that I had survived. . . .

"The woman kept her eyes glued to my face while blocking the door with her body. Her angry eyes also asked, Why did you survive? Why did you come back? Who needs you here? 'This is my home now. The Jewish homes were given to us Poles!' she shouted at me.

"'I do not want anything.' I felt like a beggar. 'I came to search for my family. Did anyone ask for me?'

"She shook her head. 'No! No!'

"'Please, let me look for pictures of my family. I want to remember them. I only want the pictures.'

"'I have no pictures. I threw them out with all the books I found.'

"I felt a stabbing pain in my heart. The

books—our secret library—they survived, and she threw them in the garbage. The witnesses of our struggle for dignity, she threw them in the garbage.

"'What did you do with the garbage? Where did you throw it?'

"The sound of my voice scared her. She stepped back a little, as if afraid I was going crazy, that I might attack her. 'It was in the yard, but some people came—some of your people—several weeks ago. They came to search for the books. All they wanted was the books.'

"I ran to the yard. Broken pieces of furniture, glass, torn books, many traces of our life were scattered over the yard in the garbage. But there were no pictures, no pictures. . . ."

"I took a last look at the place that was my home. The place I had shared with the people I loved and cherished. The place where together we had hoped, dreamed, studied, believed in a new tomorrow.

"I held onto the wall of the building, stood there crying. Then I left. I went to the cemetery to search for Laibele's grave. I found it covered with weeds. I cleared the grave carefully. I sat on the ground and talked to Laibele just as I used to when he lay in his sickbed. 'I am here with you, my little brother. Why did I come back? Why not Moishele? Why not Motele? And now I must leave. I cannot live here. This earth is soaked with our blood.'

"I sat there, staring at the bare grave. 'I must make you a tombstone, little brother. There is no one left to clear the weeds. I must make you a tombstone to keep the weeds from covering your name. Laibele Minski. Died April 1943, age 13. In the ghetto of Lodz.'

"I searched for some bricks and found a white metal headboard from a child's bed. I dragged it over to the grave and put it at the head of the grave. 'You have a new bed, little brother. Sleep, Laibele. At least you have a grave . . .'

"I cried for hours before I left. I cried for his lost young life. I cried for all those who have no grave, no traces. I cried for the lonely survivors who must go on."

Nancy touches my face softly. "But, you were lucky, Mommy. You found your sisters and a brother."

"Yes, my darling. I was lucky. I found Mala

and Chanele and Yankele. They returned from Russia. I was thirteen when we parted. I was twenty when we found one another again. We met again in the Displaced Persons camps in Germany. Finally we all came to America. Yes, I was lucky."

She smiles. "Now you have Daddy, your children, your grandchildren. You have a new life."

I hug her close to me. "I love you, Mommy, and I am sorry."

I kiss her softly. Cuddling her face in my hands, I whisper, "As long as there is life, there is hope."